The Art of Hearing

Following the Voice of God

Dag Heward-Mills

Unless otherwise stated, all Scripture quotations are taken from the King James Version of the Bible.

ISBN 10: 9988-596-10-3
ISBN 13: 978-9988-596-10-1

5th Printing 2007

Dag Heward-Mills
P. O. Box KB114
Korle-Bu, Accra
Ghana, West-Africa

Website:
www.daghewardmills.org

Email:
bishop@daghewardmills.org
evangelist@daghewardmills.org

Dedication

To
Pastor *Kingsley Gyasi*
Thank you for a great work done in South Africa.
You have laid the foundation for the salvation of many souls.

Contents

Chapter 1

Eight Areas of Your Life Which Must Be Open to the Voice of God

The voice of God is important for every area of your life. If there is anything that is important to you, I would suggest that you open that area to the direction of God's Spirit. You may think that God is not interested in certain areas of your life. I want you to know today that God has something to say about every area of your life. The Lord is depicted as a shepherd to His sheep. Sheep are animals that are very dependent on human beings for everything. If the Lord is depicted as a Shepherd, it shows how dependent we are on Him for everything.

1.   Depend on the voice of God for *your needs*.

The LORD is my shepherd; I SHALL NOT WANT.

Psalm 23:1

"I shall not want" is what you will say after you have followed the Shepherd for some time! You will be able to say with David, "I have no needs, I am blessed in every way." In order to experience this, you must follow the leading of the Spirit.

2.   Depend on the Holy Spirit for *your marriage and home*.

He maketh me to LIE DOWN IN GREEN PASTURES: he leadeth me BESIDE THE STILL WATERS.

Psalm 23:2

Green pasture speaks of peace and happiness. It speaks of the marriages we all desire. You will never have true happiness unless you marry the person God wants you to marry. If you allow Him, the Holy Spirit will lead you to a peaceful marriage.

3.   Depend on the voice of God for *the right church*.

He restoreth my soul: HE LEADETH ME in the paths of righteousness for his name's sake.

Psalm 23:3

This Scripture shows how dependent you are on God's guidance for righteous living. Many people end up as fruitless nonentities in the kingdom of God because they are under the wrong leadership. It is so important to be led by the Spirit when you are choosing a church. It makes all the difference in the world! Most definitely, this is one of the important areas where you need the guidance of the Holy Spirit.

4. Depend on the voice of God for *divine protection*.

Yea, though I walk through the valley of the shadow of death, I WILL FEAR NO EVIL: FOR THOU ART WITH ME; thy rod and thy staff they comfort me.

Psalm 23:4

The psalmist made it clear that he was dependent on the Shepherd for protection. He explained how the Lord's protection was so powerful that he was able to eat lunch when his enemy was nearby.

Listening to the news, it is almost as though travellers are playing Russian roulette. Russian roulette is a game involving the firing of a revolver, with one chamber loaded, at one's head, after spinning the chamber. If you are the unlucky one, the bullet will be fired when you pull the trigger. It is almost as though it is a game of chance for you to travel and return safely. Definitely, you need the voice of God to choose the right car, bus, plane or train!

5. Depend on the voice of God for *the Anointing*.

...thou ANOINTEST my head with oil; my cup runneth over.

Psalm 23:5

Without being directed by the Lord you will never be anointed. The anointing will not come from Heaven per se. God will have to direct you to relate with anointed men of God. Jesus told His disciples, *"Follow* me and I will *make* you…"* Without following the right person you will not amount to much in the ministry. Surely, you depend on the voice of God to lead you.

6. Depend on the voice of God for *the good things of this life.*

Surely GOODNESS and MERCY shall follow me all the days of my life:…

Psalm 23:6

Every businessman must know this reality. Without the grace of God you will never make it to the top. The silver and the gold belong to the Lord. If you seek His face, He will show you where it is hidden!

The silver is mine, and the gold is mine, saith the LORD of hosts.

Haggai 2:8

7. Depend on the voice of God *to make it to Heaven.*

…and I will DWELL IN THE HOUSE OF THE LORD FOR EVER.

Psalm 23:6

Do you want to dwell in the house of the Lord forever? As you follow the Spirit of God, He will lead you on the path of righteousness. This will eventually lead to Heaven. You need the Shepherd to take you from the green pastures all the way to those eternal gates.

8. Depend on the voice of God to *fulfil your ministry*.

...he leadeth me in the PATHS OF RIGHTEOUSNESS for his name's sake.

Psalm 23:3

You are alive on this earth to fulfil your ministry! This is the reason why God created and saved you. If you do not fulfil your ministry, you have missed your whole purpose for this life!

Chapter 2

How to Avoid Losing Your Gift

S tudying the voice of God can be a little frightening, especially when you think of the consequences that can befall you when you do not obey His voice. In this chapter, I want to share with you why every Christian or minister should obey the voice of God.

Years ago I noticed this Scripture,

For though I preach the gospel, I have nothing to glory of: for necessity is laid upon me; yea, WOE IS UNTO ME, IF I PREACH NOT THE GOSPEL!

1 Corinthians 9:16

Paul was someone who felt he would get into all sorts of trouble if he did not preach the Gospel. He was not wrong!

Indeed, I think I can say with Paul, "Woe is unto me, if I preach not the Gospel."

Every minister who does not take the leading of the Spirit seriously will open himself to all sorts of dangerous attacks. He will be in danger of losing the anointing!

A Minister Must Obey the Voice of God to Avoid Having the Gift Taken Away

And he said unto them that stood by, TAKE FROM HIM THE POUND, and give it to him that hath ten pounds.

Luke 19:24

Dear man of God, do not think that you are indispensable. If you do not do what God wants you to do, your ministry will be taken away from you and given to another. Read it for yourself! *Take from him the pound!* If God gave you a pound, He can take it back when He wants to. Pastors seem to enjoy hiding behind Romans 11:29.

For the gifts and calling of God are without repentance.

Romans 11:29

Because of this verse, they think that God will never take away His anointing. But that cannot be the case. What this Scripture means is that God does not change His mind about you. **He never changes His decision to call you or use you**. He never changes His decision to anoint you.

7

If God has called you to be a vessel, you will always be a vessel. The story of the Prophet Jonah is a good example of how God does not change His mind about the people He wants to use. Jonah did not want to go where the Lord had sent him. He wanted to be a nice guy everybody liked.

> **Now the word of the LORD came unto Jonah the son of Amittai, saying, Arise, go to Nineveh, that great city, and cry against it; for their wickedness is come up before me. But Jonah rose up to flee unto Tarshish from the presence of the LORD, and went down to Joppa; and he found a ship going to Tarshish: so he paid the fare thereof, and went down into it, to go with them unto Tarshish from the presence of the LORD. But the LORD sent out a great wind into the sea, and there was a mighty tempest in the sea, so that the ship was like to be broken.**
>
> **Jonah 1:1-4**

However, when the season of grace is over, God will have no choice but to recall His pound. He may have to give this pound to another minister, hoping that one would be faithful.

Will You Write This Book?

I remember a man of God whom the Lord spoke to about writing a book. The Lord asked him, "Will you write this book?"

He said, "Yes Lord, of course I will!"

And the Lord said, "I hope so, because you are the fifth person I have asked. If you do not write it, I will move on to the sixth person."

Dear friend, in this story you see two principles working together. On one hand, God does not change His mind about writing the book. On the other, God is forced to select someone else and give him the job.

Yes, I believe that God does not change His mind about us. But I also know that God can recall His pound and give it to another.

And he said unto them that stood by, TAKE FROM HIM the pound, and GIVE IT TO HIM THAT hath ten pounds.

Luke 19:24

Keep the gift of God by obeying His call! Be sensitive to His voice! Do what He tells you to do and you will succeed in ministry! Do what is hard and difficult rather than what is nice and easy!

Chapter 3

How to Avoid Premature Death

And cast ye the unprofitable servant into outer darkness: there shall be weeping and gnashing of teeth.

Matthew 25:30

The expression "weeping and gnashing of teeth" is a little misunderstood by most of us. We often think it refers to Hell and Hades. However, the Bible does not explicitly say that the people it refers to will go to Hell. It says that they will weep and gnash their teeth in darkness. Weeping speaks of sorrow and of pain associated with funerals. This Scripture could be warning all who claim to be servants of God that failure to obey could cost them their very lives.

A Minister Must Obey the Voice of God to Avoid Weeping and Gnashing of Teeth

Kenneth Hagin, a great prophet I deeply respect, often spoke of how ministers die before their time because they do not obey the Lord concerning their ministry. He spoke of how he broke his arm and was admitted to the hospital. When the Lord Jesus appeared to him in the hospital, he discovered that his accident had occurred because he did not take an aspect of his ministry seriously.

Dear friend, doing the work of God is not a joke. It is not a game! People were made to experience weeping and gnashing of teeth because they were unprofitable. "Unprofitable" simply means *"unbeneficial, running at a loss, unsuccessful and losing money* (souls)". When you are losing souls for the Lord, do not expect Him to be pleased with you. He may have to recall or replace you.

I remember a testimony given by the pastor of one of the world's largest churches. He described how he was rummaging through some old pictures. He noticed a picture that was taken during his Bible school days. There were about fifty people in his class. As he mused over the picture, he realized that about forty-five of his classmates were dead. He then remembered that the five who were still alive, were the only ones who were serious about prayer during their Bible school days. He also realized that they were the only ones who took the ministry seriously after Bible school. Many of the others had taken to other professions.

Dear friend, ministry is serious business. God does not take lightly the investment that He places in you. To whom much is given, much is required!

>...For unto whomsoever much is given, of him shall be much required...

Luke 12:48

If you desert the army during wartime, your punishment is often execution.   Everyone who withholds his gifts and abilities in a time of war is cursed.

>**Cursed be he that doeth the work of the LORD deceitfully, and cursed be he that keepeth back his sword from blood.**

Jeremiah 48:10

The Young Prophet Meets His Untimely Death

And, behold, there came a man of God out of Judah by the word of the LORD unto Bethel: and Jeroboam stood by the altar to burn incense. And he cried against the altar in the word of the LORD, and said, O altar, altar, thus saith the LORD; Behold, a child shall be born unto the house of David, Josiah by name; and upon thee shall he offer the priests of the high places that burn incense upon thee, and men's bones shall be burnt upon thee. And he gave a sign the same day, saying, This is the sign which the LORD hath spoken; Behold, the altar shall be rent, and the ashes that are upon it shall be poured out.

And it came to pass, when king Jeroboam heard the saying of the man of God, which had cried against the altar in Bethel, that he put forth his hand from the altar, saying, Lay hold on him. And his hand, which he put forth against him, dried up, so that he could not pull it in again to him. The altar also was

12

rent, and the ashes poured out from the altar, according to the sign which the man of God had given by the word of the LORD. And the king answered and said unto the man of God, Intreat now the face of the LORD thy God, and pray for me, that my hand may be restored me again. And the man of God besought the LORD, and the king's hand was restored him again, and became as it was before. And the king said unto the man of God, Come home with me, and refresh thyself, and I will give thee a reward.

And the man of God said unto the king, if thou wilt give me half thine house, I will not go in with thee, neither will I eat bread nor drink water in this place: For so was it charged me by the word of the LORD, saying, Eat no bread, nor drink water, nor turn again by the same way that thou camest. So he went another way, and returned not by the way that he came to Bethel.

Now there dwelt an old prophet in Bethel; and his sons came and told him all the works that the man of God had done that day in Bethel: the words which he had spoken unto the king, them they told also to their father. And their father said unto them, What way went he? For his sons had seen what way the man of God went, which came from Judah. And he said unto his sons, Saddle me the ass. So they saddled him the ass: and he rode thereon; And went after the man of God, and found him sitting under an oak: and he said unto him, Art thou the man of God that camest from Judah? And he said, I am. Then he said unto him, Come home with me, and eat bread. And he said, I may not return with thee, nor go in with thee: neither will I eat bread or drink water with thee in this place: For it was said to me by the word of the LORD, Thou shalt eat no bread nor drink water there, nor turn again to go by the way that thou camest.

He said unto him, I am a prophet also as thou art; and an angel spake unto me by the word of the LORD, saying, Bring him back with thee into thine house, that he may eat bread and drink water. But he lied unto him. So he went back with him, and did eat bread in his house, and drank water.

And it came to pass, as they sat at the table, that the word of the Lord came unto the prophet that brought him back: And he cried unto the man of God that came from Judah, saying, Thus saith the LORD, Foreasmuch as thou hast disobeyed the mouth of the LORD, and hast not kept the commandment which the LORD thy God commanded thee, But camest back, and hast eaten bread and drunk water in the place, of the which the LORD did say to thee, Eat no bread, and drink no water; thy carcase shall not come unto the sepulchre of thy fathers.

And it came to pass, after he had eaten bread, and after he had drunk, that he saddled for him the ass, to wit, for the prophet whom he had brought back. And when he was gone, a lion met him by the way, and slew him: and his carcase was cast in the way, and the ass stood by it, the lion also stood by the carcase. And, behold, men passed by, and saw the

carcase cast in the way, and the lion standing by the carcase: and they came and told it in the city where the old prophet dwelt.

And when the prophet that brought him back from the way heard thereof, he said, It is the man of God, who was disobedient unto the word of the LORD: therefore the LORD hath delivered him unto the lion, which hath torn him, and slain him, according to the word of the LORD, which he spake unto him.

1 Kings 13:1-26

A Minister Must Obey the Voice of God to Avoid Premature Death

In this story, the Lord specifically told the prophet what to do. By obeying the voice of God this man of God became a worker of signs and wonders. He suddenly had a thriving ministry. Then here comes an old and backslidden man of God. Did you know that men of God can also backslide? Unfortunately, this younger prophet listened to another "voice".

At a certain level of ministry, you may become confused by the different voices that are trying to guide you. Make sure that you stick with the Word of God.

In the New Testament, Paul explicitly stated that people were sick and *dead* because they did not discern the Lord's Body. Paul gave the reason for disease and death in the church.

For he that eateth and drinketh unworthily, eateth and drinketh damnation to himself, not discerning the Lord's body. For this cause MANY ARE WEAK and SICKLY among you, and MANY SLEEP [DEAD].

1 Corinthians 11:29,30

To discern the Lord's Body means to realize or discern that you are dealing with the Lord's Body. All the sheep and little lambs are the Lord's Body. They are the ones He died for on the cross.

If for instance, you knew that somebody's finger was on the table, you would not strike it with a big hammer. You would not hit that finger because you know it is part of his body.

When you fail to realize that the church is Christ's Body, you will get into trouble. Those sheep, those people, are the ones the Lord shed His blood for! They are His body! When you abandon them, it is like abandoning your mouth (a part of your body) by not brushing your teeth for months. You can imagine why the Lord gets mad at ministers who neglect His Body.

Chapter 4

How to Avoid Being Replaced

J esus died for the little lambs. He told us to "go!" He told us to feed His little lambs. One day, the Lord became very angry with His shepherds. Look at what He said to them. He said He would take over and shepherd the people Himself.

Therefore, ye shepherds, hear the word of the LORD; As I live, saith the Lord GOD, surely because my flock became a prey, and my flock became meat to every beast of the field, because there was no shepherd, neither did my shepherds search for my flock, but the shepherds fed themselves, and fed not my flock; Thus saith the Lord GOD; Behold, I am against the shepherds; and I will require my flock at their hand, and cause them

to cease from feeding the flock; neither shall the shepherds feed themselves any more; for I will deliver my flock from their mouth, that they may not be meat for them. **FOR THUS SAITH THE LORD GOD; BEHOLD, I, EVEN I, WILL BOTH SEARCH MY SHEEP, AND SEEK THEM OUT.**

Ezekiel 34:7,8,10,11

One night, while in a hotel in South America, the Lord spoke to me about His work. I had never heard the Lord speak so mournfully as He did that night. He spoke of how nobody cared about His work. He told me that everyone was running about his or her own business. He said to me, "No one cares about my work." I found this very sad but real.

When we do not obey the Lord, we are in effect neglecting His sheep. Jesus asked Peter whether he would feed the sheep. Peter was taken aback, wondering why the Lord was asking. "After three years of training what do you expect me to do?" he must have thought. But the Lord knew how many ministers would abandon His work!

A Minister Must Obey the Voice of God to Avoid Being Displaced and Replaced

When a minister neglects or abandons God's work, the Lord gets angry. This is the reason why He often displaces and replaces men of God with new ones.

A Vision of Replacement

One day I had a strange vision. In this vision, I saw a man being lifted from his chair by the collar of his neck. I did not see who the man was. Suddenly, I found myself being lifted by the collar of *my* neck and being placed in *his* chair.

After that the Lord told me that I was replacing someone in the ministry.

Dear friend, I tell you, I was frightened! I was not frightened about replacing someone but rather because the reality that I could also be replaced one day, became very real to me! This vision was very biblical because it happened many times in the Scriptures.

Samuel replaced Eli! David replaced Saul! Elisha replaced Elijah!

...and Elisha the son of Shaphat of Abel-meholah shalt thou anoint to be prophet IN THY ROOM.

1 Kings 19:16

You have a room (place) in the ministry. However, it is not a permanent room. It can be given to anyone who deserves it. Always remember that there are people ready to replace you if you do not obey the voice of God. Obey the voice of God to avoid replacement!

Chapter 5

Twelve Kinds of Voices Every Christian Should Know About

There are, it may be, so MANY KINDS OF VOICES in the world, and none of them is without signification.

1 Corinthians 14:10

O ne of the greatest desires of all serious Christians is to know the will of God. With a little experience in life, anyone can tell that there are many different ways your life can go. We often come to the crossroads and ask, "Which way is best?" If you take the wrong road, the implications may be devastating. If you marry the wrongperson, the consequences may be terrible. If you join the wrong church, the consequences may be eternal.

Many times when we take decisions, we are unable to retrace our steps. In other words, many decisions are irreversible. Because of this, we need to know the will of God so that we can be guided along every step of the way.

Even Unbelievers Want to Know the Future

Unbelievers have ways of getting to know what is best for them. Many of them consult soothsayers, astrologers and fortune tellers. They put their trust in false prophets and occult power. They also see the need to know what to do next. African politicians are often said to consult these powers on a regular basis. They often ask for direction and protection from them. African soccer teams consult these mediums as well. You will notice however, that none of these things have taken them very far.

As Christians, we do not need to consult satanic powers to know the future. God has graciously given us the Holy Spirit to guide us. Being led by the Spirit of God is a sign that you are a true Christian.

For as many as are led by the Spirit of God, they are the sons of God.

Romans 8:14

In the Old Testament, only the prophet seemed to know the will of God. You see, the Holy Spirit was not given to everyone at that time. We are living in a blessed dispensation. We all have the Holy Spirit in us and can be led by the Spirit of God. It is possible for us to know the will of God. That is what this book is all about:

"How to know the will of God" and "How to be led by the Spirit of God."

Twelve Different Kinds of Voices

The first step to knowing the will of God is to recognize that there are many types of voices in this world and all of them are trying to influence you. The art of selecting the right voice and listening to that voice is the art of being led by the Spirit of God.

God wants to deliver you from evil and He has sent His Spirit to lead you through this life so that you will not make tragic mistakes.

Satan, who is God's opponent and an opposition party, is trying to lead you in the wrong way or at least confuse you. What are the voices that are trying to influence you? There are several possibilities that you must be aware of:

1. ~ The voice of God ~
2. ~ The voice of the flesh ~
3. ~ The voice of the mind ~
4. ~ The voice of the devil ~
5. ~ The voice of a prophet ~
6. ~ The voice of your pastor ~
7. ~ The voice of your friends ~
8. ~ The voice of your parents ~
9. ~ The voice of your spirit ~
10. ~ The voice of your spouse ~
11. ~ The voice of circumstances ~
12. ~ The voice of your own will ~

All these voices, as well as some others, are probably in operation in your life. Depending on who you are, you may be influenced more or less by these voices. A young man may claim that the voice of God spoke to him, directing him to marry a beautiful young lady in the church. He may approach the young woman and tell her, "God spoke to me last night." Is this young man telling the truth? Did he really hear the voice of God?

Let me make an important point here. There are at least twelve different voices that this young man could have heard. He could have heard the voice of circumstances leading him to marry this young lady or he could have heard the voice of his flesh, desirous of the opposite sex. He could also have genuinely heard the voice of God. None of these voices is without significance. What is important is to know which voice is leading you.

The Thirsty Donkey

I always remember the story of a thirsty donkey that went on a long journey through the desert. At the end of his tedious journey, the donkey was tired, hungry and thirsty. As it trudged along, it noticed two stacks of hay at different ends of the field. The donkey thought to himself, "There is food for me!" Then he realized that the two different haystacks were at opposite ends of an extremely large field.

The donkey, being a "Christian", decided to seek the will of God concerning which of the haystacks he should approach. The donkey decided to pray. As the donkey was bowing his head to pray, he noticed a bucket of water positioned by the haystack on the right. The donkey then prayed a simple but powerful prayer and said, "O God, I want to know your will concerning which direction to go. Should I go to the haystack on the right or to the one on the left?"

After praying, the donkey gathered himself together and began to walk towards one of the haystacks. Which of the stacks of hay do you think the donkey went to? The stack on the right or that on the left? Well, when the donkey was asked he said, "God has directed me to the one on the right."

Everyone can predict that the donkey would say that God had directed him to the haystack on the right. However, you and I both know that it was probably the bucket of water that attracted the donkey to the haystack on the right. **It is time to be honest! It is time to tell the truth! Is it really the Spirit of God who is leading us or is it the voice of our flesh and of circumstances?**

Anytime someone claims to have been directed by the "Spirit of God", you should remember that there are over twelve different possibilities that exist. The voice he claims to be hearing is one out of twelve or more different voices. Is it the voice of his friends? Is it the voice of his wife? Is it the voice of circumstances? What is actually leading this person?

Three in One Day!

I learnt of a man who became close to three Christian sisters at the same time. This man happened to be in Bible school at the same time with these three ladies who were his age. They attended classes together, they prayed together and they even went to church together. As time passed, they became a very closely knit family. There was a real flow of Christian love and friendship among them. This Christian brother was a very caring young man. He was also handsome and was obviously a promising minister. He was good at the ministry of counselling and seemed to be a patient listener to people's problems.

At the end of the course, something interesting happened! It was graduation time and each of the three Christian sisters approached this compassionate brother with a "message" from the Lord. Each one of them said (unknown to the others), "God has spoken to me about you that we should spend the rest of our lives and ministries together." In other words, God had supposedly spoken to each of these women to marry the brother. The brother was so surprised. He told them, "I appreciate your sharing this with me, but God hasn't spoken to me about this." He did not marry any of these three girls. He ended up marrying somebody else.

I find this true story very interesting. It illustrates the point I am trying to make. Each of these three ladies claimed to have heard the voice of God. But as I said, there are several possibilities to each claim. How could God tell three different people, at the same time, to marry one man? Does His Word not tell us that God wants one man to marry only one woman?

They were obviously hearing the voice of their own flesh. It could be the voice of their minds. They claimed that the voice of their flesh was the voice of God. These three ladies embarrassed themselves. You can save yourself from embarrassment when you learn to distinguish between the voice of the Spirit and other voices. That is what this book is all about – how to know the voice of God and how to follow the Holy Spirit to the top! In the following chapters, I will share some things about these different voices and how you can distinguish between them.

Chapter 6

Four Things Every Christian Should Know about the Voice of the Mind

And the very God of peace sanctify you wholly; and I pray God your whole SPIRIT and SOUL and BODY be preserved blameless unto the coming of our Lord Jesus Christ.

1 Thessalonians 5:23

Man consists of a spirit, a soul and a body. That is quite clear from the verse above. Each of these components of the human being has a voice.

Your thought processes and your reasoning are the voice of your mind. God never intended for us to do away with our minds. Many people stop reasoning and thinking when they become Christians. There is a funny notion that it is wrong to reason or understand things once you are in the kingdom of God. There is a feeling that if you are a spiritual person it is not right to reason things out. This has led to many disasters in this life.

Four Things Every Christian Should Know about the Voice of the Mind

1. The mind is a great asset for every Christian and every minister.

I believe that the mind is one of the most wonderful gifts that God has given to every man. The mind is one of the most complex computers in the world today. It is a gift that you are expected to use. Even when you are born-again, you are expected to use your mind. When you are a spiritual leader, you are expected to use your mind!

When you want to decide whether to marry someone or not, you must first use your mind. You must ask yourself, "What is the background of this person? How old is he or she? What is the educational background of the person? What is the family background of the person? What language does he or she speak?"

The Difference between Men and Animals

When I have to take decisions in the ministry, I do not just pray about them. I think about them! I analyse things! God gave me a mind and I intend to use it on a daily basis. What is the difference between a human being and an animal? The human being has a more developed brain. This gives him a mind with a great thinking capability. It is the use of the mind, which has made human beings rule and dominate all animals.

We human beings have control over animals that are wild and dangerous. We control poisonous and deadly reptiles by the use of a superior mind. We capture animals like elephants and whales that are a hundred times the size of a man. We keep them in cages and observe them at our pleasure. What gives us this power? It is the use of a superior mind.

The Difference between Men and Men

Even amongst human beings, those that have encouraged the use of the mind have ended up ruling those that have not used their minds much. The educated (developed minds) are ruling the uneducated. Go into almost every institution and you will find that the educated are higher placed than the uneducated. They have higher salaries and are better looked after.

In a very sophisticated world, the inventors of cars and airplanes are dominating millions of people who have not used their minds to create such things. The inventors and manufacturers of televisions, videos and telephones have more money than those who just buy and use them. Through the world's complex financial system, many people who are officially free from slavery are still experiencing a sophisticated form of financial and mental slavery!

Those who know how to convert cocoa beans into chocolate and other niceties have more "say so" than those who just know how to harvest cocoa on a farm. It takes more use of the mind to develop machines and complicated equipment that are used to convert raw materials into final products.

Simply speaking, the world is divided into two: those who have used their God-given gift of a super mind and those who have not!

2.   Do not send your mind on vacation because you have become a spiritual person.

Do a survey of some churches.   Those who have emphasized on spiritual and emotional things, to the absolute exclusion of rational thinking, have ended up on the rocks. God does not expect you to exclude your mind because you are a spiritual person. I consider myself to be a very spiritual person. I spend numerous hours a week in prayer. I believe that the Bible is my final authority on all matters of doctrine. This however, has not made me to stop reasoning and rationalizing things. When you stop using your mind, even in the spiritual world, you lower yourself from the rank that God intends for you.

How to Cross a Road

Someone wanted to know the will of God about marriage. I said to him, "Do you know the Kaneshie-Mallam Highway (a very wide and dangerous highway in the city of Accra in my country, Ghana)?"

He said, "Yes, I do."

I asked him, "If you wanted to cross that road what would you do?"

He began to answer but I stopped him.

I said to him, "I know what you would do! You would close your eyes and ask the Lord to speak to you and tell you the exact moment to cross."

He smiled.

I continued, "Wouldn't you do that?"

"I don't think so," he responded.

I went on, "If you were to do something like that you are likely to be killed immediately. The highest form of manifested stupidity is to shut off your mind when you are taking important decisions."

I said to him, "God is not the author of foolishness. He does not expect you to close your eyes and listen to the voice of the Spirit telling you when to cross. He gave you eyes to see and a mind with which to make sound judgements. It is like having money in your pocket that God has given you to solve your problems. Yet, you cry to Him and ask Him for money. Meanwhile, you have some money in your pocket.

What is God saying to you? God is saying that it is time to think again. It is time to be educated. It is time to reason. If you are a pastor, do not take all the decisions on your own. When it comes to finances, think and use the minds of trained accountants. When it comes to legal matters, believe and accept the minds of trained lawyers. When it comes to church growth, read and learn everything you can.

3.   A combination of the voice of the Spirit and the voice of the mind will lead to your promotion in life and ministry.

The Holy Spirit is not the author of foolishness and absurdities. Please stop claiming that the Spirit is telling you things when that is not the case! There are many things that I do not pray about; I simply *think* about them. The Bible says that Christ is to us not only power but also wisdom.

...Christ the power of God, and the WISDOM OF GOD.

1 Corinthians 1:24

Jesus Christ in our lives makes us wise and not foolish. If you want to be promoted in this life, get wisdom. Wisdom has to do with the mind. The Bible says that wisdom is the principal thing. Therefore, with all your getting, get wisdom.

Exalt her [wisdom], and she shall promote thee: she shall bring thee to honour, when thou dost embrace her.

Proverbs 4:8

Your promotion and honour are on the way when you start applying yourself to God's wisdom. Never forget that it was wisdom that brought Joseph out of jail and into the king's palace. Wisdom brought Daniel into the rank of prime minister and vice-president in three successive governments. It was wisdom and the use of his mind that made Solomon the richest man on earth. **Wisdom is the intelligent use of your thinking capabilities. Wisdom is the ability to take right decisions based on the information available to you. Wisdom is the ability *not* to ignore realities when they are before you.**

4.   Too much reasoning can turn you into a fool.

There is, however, one danger with the voice of the mind–the danger of reasoning until you become foolish again. Knowledge and thinking without God will make you into a fool.

The expositors of the evolution theory reasoned their way through a maze of obvious scientific realities involving the evolution of created beings. They saw some things and propounded some theories. However, when they got to a point where they had to question themselves about the *origin* of all created beings, they began to guess and made fools out of themselves.

It is the mother of all absurdities for someone to say that this intricate, fantastic and perfect creation of God came about through an explosion (The Big Bang Theory). In the medical school, I dissected the body of a dead human being for one and a half years. I discovered for myself how extraordinary and awesome God's creation is.

This is why the Bible says it is only a fool who says that there is no God. No one can tell me that an explosion that occurred in Germany created a Mercedes-Benz car. That is foolishness!

Even though you must develop your mind, God's Word and His Spirit are superior to every reasoning of man. You must allow the wisdom of God to supersede the wisdom of man.

Where is the wise? where is the scribe? where is the disputer of this world? hath not God made foolish the wisdom of this world?

1 Corinthians 1:20

Because the foolishness of God is wiser than men; and the weakness of God is stronger than men.

1 Corinthians 1:25

There are times when God will direct you and it will not look wise in the natural. When I left my noble medical profession for the Ministry, many people thought I had gone mad. My parents were distressed and my relatives were worried. They could not see the sense in what I was doing.

They asked, "Why should someone leave such a promising career for an apparently fruitless and uncertain adventure?"

But I knew that God had called me and at such times natural reasoning had to give way to the voice of God.

The problem with this is that many Christians are simply not using their minds at all. They continue claiming that every quixotic adventure they embark on is directed by the supernatural voice of God.

It is time to let the voice of your mind have its proper place.

Chapter 7

Five Keys to Victory over the Voice of Your Flesh

Remember These Keys

1. The voice of your flesh is your human desire.

2. The voice of your flesh is your physical feelings.

3. The voice of the flesh says, "Do what feels nice and easy."

4. Do not obey the voice of the flesh if you want to be blessed.

5. You can silence the voice of the flesh by doing what is hard and difficult.

The voice of your flesh is the expression of your desires and feelings. Whenever you have certain feelings and desires, the flesh is speaking. The flesh is a very dangerous thing to follow. If you follow your desires for food, rest and sex, you will end up as a spiritual disaster.

FOR TO BE CARNALLY MINDED IS DEATH; but to be spiritually minded is life and peace.

Romans 8:6

A spiritual person is someone who grows to the point where he is able to realize when his flesh is speaking or influencing him. Jesus said, "The spirit is willing but the flesh is weak" (Matthew 26:41). The flesh always wants to do the wrong thing. It constantly influences you along the course of least resistance.

I have realized that if I do the things that are hard and difficult, I get to be promoted. Whereas, if I do the things which are nice and easy, I do not progress. The flesh wants you to sleep. It is your flesh that will say to you, "Do not go to that all-night prayer meeting."

Many young men should know that it is actually the desire of the flesh that motivates them towards marriage and relationships. Often, young men are not led by the Spirit into marriage but by their flesh!

A Special Ministry

Some years ago, as a student in Achimota School (a secondary school in Ghana), I noticed a young man who called himself a minister. He would come to the school to visit us and to minister the Word.

After a while, I observed that this man hardly ever visited the brothers in the boarding school. He could always be found chatting with the ladies and "ministering" to them. One day I asked him, "How come you hardly come to see the brothers anymore?"

I added, "You spend all your time at the girls' dormitory."

"Oh," he answered, "I have a special call from God. My ministry is to the sisters."

In other words, God had called him to spend all his time with the ladies.

At that time, I accepted it as a valid ministry. However, if you study the Bible, you will not find such a ministry. The Bible says that the older women should teach the younger women (Titus 2:4).

This fellow was probably just following the natural dictates of his flesh. As a man, he tended to flow more with the sisters. This is a natural phenomenon. It happens all the time. But instead of acknowledging the reality of his flesh and what was natural, he claimed that the Holy Spirit had given him a *special ministry* to girls.

The "Spirit" Speaks?

A young man was sent out by the General Superintendent of his denomination to pioneer a church in the metropolis. This young man was poorly educated and had no steady job. He was however operating as a lay pastor (an unpaid/voluntary minister). He began the church by witnessing and following-up the converts. To his surprise, the church began to grow. The church's growth was aided by the good name of that ministry. He also flowed in the general anointing that was over that denomination.

The church that had begun in the young man's sitting room, soon grew until there were over one hundred members in the church. The money began to roll in and for the first time, the church's bank account had over one million cedis (five hundred dollars at the 1999 exchange rate). After a while, the man who said that the church should meet in his house free of charge came up with an outrageous sum, as rent owed him. This pastor had obviously seen the financial capacity and capability of the church. The church had more money than he thought it would ever have.

The denomination's administrators however, refused to pay that huge sum of money. They offered to pay a smaller sum of money. The rent issue then died a natural death. However, a couple of months later the pastor suddenly requested an audience with the General Superintendent of the church.

"What can we do for you?" the Superintendent asked.

"The Lord has spoken to me. He has asked me to resign from this ministry and to begin my own church," the pastor revealed.

The surprised Superintendent queried, "What do you mean?"

"It's nothing personal. God has called me. He said I should start my own ministry."

"I see," said the Superintendent, "Are you sure there is no other reason?"

"No! The Spirit of God has spoken and I have to obey!"

The administrators of the church questioned this pastor, "Is it not because you want control over the church's money? Are you not taking this decision for financial reasons?"

37

The pastor was not pleased, "Are you doubting my call? Do you doubt that God has spoken to me?"

This pastor eventually took over the church, changed its name and stole the entire congregation. The denomination decided to start another church nearby for those of its members who wanted to remain loyal to the denomination.

A week after this pastor had stolen the congregation, it came to light that he had been siphoning money from the church offerings. Instead of following the clearly laid down rules of his denomination (to bank all monies immediately), he would take some money out and use it. In other words, he was making wrong declarations of the church's offerings.

This is an example of someone who claimed that he had heard the voice of God. Although no one can really judge, it is quite obvious that there were many financial considerations in this young pastor's decision to break away from his denomination.

The voice of the flesh crying out for more money was being heard loud and clear. Learn to distinguish the voice of the flesh from other voices.

There are, it may be, so MANY KINDS OF VOICES in the world, and none of them is without signification.

1 Corinthians 14:10

Chapter 8

Three Important Truths about the Voice of the Holy Spirit

The voice of the Holy Spirit is the most important voice that we need to hear in these times. Jesus said that He would send us the Holy Spirit to guide us. The Holy Spirit speaks the mind of God.

> **...for he shall not speak of himself; but whatsoever he shall hear, that shall he speak: and he will shew you things to come.**
>
> **John 16:13**

1. The voice of the Holy Spirit transmits God's current plan for you.

One of the cardinal duties of the Holy Spirit is to transmit God's mind to you. He will not speak of Himself. Whatever He hears God say, He will relay it to you. From today, there is no need to consult the astrologers or the stars. The Holy Spirit will show you things to come.

God will tell you what to expect. If He does not tell you anything, then there is nothing unusual to expect. The Holy Spirit is on duty twenty-four hours a day; He speaks all the time. It is our duty therefore to learn about His voice and how to distinguish it from other voices.

2. The Holy Spirit may choose to speak to your spirit, soul or body.

The Holy Spirit has a voice. However, the Bible teaches that He speaks directly to your spirit, soul or body. **When the Holy Spirit speaks to your mind, it will sound a little different from when He speaks to your physical body.**

I have experienced the voice of the Holy Spirit speaking to me in all three ways. He speaks to us in all three ways and it is important for us to receive from the Holy Spirit in whichever way He chooses to speak to us. When the Holy Spirit speaks to your spirit, you do not hear an audible voice. This is what people call "the inner witness".

3. The voice of the Holy Spirit to your spirit is called the "Inner Witness".

The Bible also tells us that the Holy Spirit is in our hearts (spirit) crying "Abba Father", which is the cry of a child to his real father. By the voice of the Holy Spirit in your heart, you know that you are a real child of God.

And because ye are sons, God hath sent forth THE SPIRIT of his Son into your hearts, CRYING, Abba, Father.

Galatians 4:6

This verse says that the Holy Spirit is crying or shouting in your heart. But have you ever heard an audible voice saying "Abba Father"? Have you ever had an audible voice flashing through your mind saying "Abba Father"? The answer is no! What is the effect of the Holy Spirit crying "Abba Father" in our heart? It creates a silent assurance of your salvation. You know that you are a Christian and you know that you are going to Heaven.

The voice of the Holy Spirit to your spirit creates what I call a *quiet assurance*. It creates a *relaxed knowing* about something. Apostle Paul described this as *perceiving* or *a knowing*. You may ask, "Pastor, how do you know these things?" I know it from the Bible. Let us read it together.

Now when much time was spent, and when sailing was now dangerous, because the fast was now already past, Paul admonished them, And said unto them, Sirs, I PERCEIVE that this voyage will be with hurt and much damage, not only of the lading and ship, but also of our lives. Nevertheless the centurion believed the master and the owner of the ship, more than those things which were spoken by Paul.

Acts 27:9-11

Apostle Paul declared to the Centurion and other experienced sailors that he *perceived* that there were going to be serious problems during the journey. Paul did not say that he had heard the Spirit of God telling him not to travel. He

just had a *knowing* and a *perception*. How did he know this?
How did he perceive this? Was it a natural perception or a
spiritual perception? It was definitely not a natural perception
because in the natural there was no sign of danger. The wind
was blowing very softly, which was a good sign.

**And when THE SOUTH WIND BLEW SOFTLY,
supposing that they had obtained their purpose,
loosing thence, they sailed close by Crete.**

Acts 27:13

As you can see, the south wind was blowing softly. There
was no indication of trouble. Paul had what many Christians
have when the Holy Spirit speaks to their spirit – *a perception
and a knowing*. As if to distinguish between the different
ways in which the Holy Spirit speaks, the Lord spoke to Paul
in a different way on this same journey.

The bad things he had perceived had happened and the
people on the ship had given up hope of surviving. However,
God spoke to Paul in an unusual or spectacular way.

**But after long abstinence Paul stood forth in the
midst of them, and said, Sirs, ye should have
hearkened unto me, and not have loosed from Crete,
and to have gained this harm and loss. And now I
exhort you to be of good cheer: for there shall be no
loss of any man's life among you, but of the ship.
For THERE STOOD BY ME THIS NIGHT THE
ANGEL OF GOD, whose I am, and whom I serve,
Saying, Fear not, Paul; thou must be brought before
Caesar: and, lo, God hath given thee all them that
sail with thee. Wherefore, sirs, be of good cheer: for
I believe God, that it shall be even as it was told me.**

Acts 27:21-25

42

You can see from this passage that the Holy Spirit spoke in two different ways on two different occasions. The first time was by the inner witness and the second time was by an angel.

Another Scripture which says the same thing is Romans 8:16.

> **The Spirit itself beareth witness with our spirit, that we are the children of God:**
>
> **Romans 8:16**

When the Holy Spirit speaks to your spirit, you do not have thoughts flashing through your mind. **The Spirit bearing witness is the same as the Spirit speaking or witnessing to your heart that you are a child of God.** This is the commonest way that you will detect the voice of the Spirit. When you want to take a decision, watch out for that quiet assurance in your heart! If you want to marry somebody, watch out for that relaxed *knowing* that "this is it!" If you need to change your job or enter a partnership, check up on whether you have that quiet assurance of peace in your heart.

The spirit itself bears witness with our spirit, that we are the children of God.

Romans 8:16

Chapter 9

Seven Characteristics of the Inner Witness

The Spirit itself BEARETH WITNESS WITH OUR SPIRIT, that we are the children of God:

Romans 8:16

And because ye are sons, God hath sent forth THE SPIRIT of his Son into your hearts, CRYING, Abba, Father.

Galatians 4:6

The question is, "How can I distinguish the voice of this inner witness? Are there any features that I must look out for? What differentiates the inner witness from an ordinary thought?" I want to give you seven characteristics that you must look out for.

1.   The inner witness is different from reasoning thoughts.

It is not mental knowledge or logical reasoning. If what you are having is just an ingenious idea, then it's probably not the inner witness

2.   The inner witness is not a physical feeling.

Because the inner witness is the voice of the Holy Spirit to your spirit, you will not have a physical feeling per se. If someone claims that he has a physical feeling in his big toe or his liver, that is probably not the inner witness!

3.   The inner witness is best identified by eliminating other voices.

A great secret to identifying the inner witness is to eliminate other voices. Ensure that it is not your flesh that wants to do something. Make sure that it is not just a reasonable proposition. There may be some good reason and some good feelings when the Spirit is leading you, but make sure it is not *just* that!

4.   The inner witness is an *impression* of peace.

The inner witness is an awareness of peace. It is the peace of God that is beyond (passes) understanding, reasoning, logic and physical things. As you develop spiritually you will become aware of the peace of God as a method of direction. You will say, "I don't have peace about this!" At other times you will say, "Even though it sounds odd, I have peace about this issue. I know it shall be well with me."

5.   The inner witness is a strong conviction.

The inner witness makes you certain about what the Lord is saying. You begin to have a quiet assurance and confidence about the will of God.

Once again, this is not easily explained. Do you think people who give up their lives for the Gospel can explain what they are doing? You cannot easily explain the faith you have! You cannot always explain the convictions you have!

6.   The inner witness is repetitive.

The inner witness is the repeated voice of the Holy Spirit speaking to your heart.

...the Spirit...crying,...

Galatians 4:6

As the Spirit cries continually, it creates an impression in you. You begin to have a conviction about certain things. You begin to know that you know. One characteristic that I have noticed is that the voice of the Spirit is repeated over and over. This happens over several weeks, months and even years.

7.   The inner witness is an inexplicable knowing.

After you have heard the voice of the Spirit several times, you begin to know what to do. It creates in you "a knowing". Sometimes people ask me, "How did you know what to do?" Sometimes all I can say is, "I just knew."

Chapter 10

How to Use "Peace the Umpire" for Daily Guidance

Paul described the phenomenon of the inner witness in a peculiar way. He called the peace of God "an umpire". In other words, we have a special referee in our lives who guides us.

And let the PEACE of God RULE in your hearts,...
Colossians 3:15

The peace of God in our hearts is supposed to rule or guide us. The peace of God in our hearts is generated by the voice of the Holy Spirit speaking to our hearts. When you don't have that peace, please be careful of danger. The Greek word translated "rule" is the word *brabeuo*. It means "to be an umpire", "to arbitrate", "to direct" and "to govern".

God is using peace to direct and govern you. I say to you, "If you don't have peace, don't go! If you don't have peace about him, don't marry him!" Peace is the umpire you have! When the umpire blows the whistle, you are supposed to stop.

It is the umpire who tells you to "play on". He signals to you when something is wrong. If you learn to follow this peace in your heart, you will experience success in all decisions that you take.

A friend of mine left church one evening and stopped a taxi on a motorway. He told me later of a terrible experience he had. He said, "I remember that as I was getting into the car I felt very uneasy. I had no peace." You see, peace the umpire was blowing the whistle and telling him, "No! Don't go!"

He narrated, "There was one person in addition to the driver. I was sitting on the back seat."

In the middle of the journey the driver began to drive very slowly. He turned off his lights and began to sing a hymn, *"Lead kindly light"(a song that is often sang at funerals)*. The driver revealed himself to be a wizard who was operating from a town near the capital, Accra. As they drove along, the driver and the man in front said to my friend, "We are taking you somewhere."

He was terrified. They turned off the motorway onto a dusty road and drove into a cemetery. When they arrived at the cemetery they told him, "Get out of the car. You are going to die."

My friend said to me, "I knew that this was my last hour. They said that they were going to sacrifice me and use parts of my body for rituals."

He continued, "Just before they were about to sacrifice me, I prayed, knowing that these were my last minutes on earth."

The driver of the car then said, "If you will join our witchcraft group, I will not kill you."

My friend told me, "I agreed to join for the sake of my life."

Thinking that they had got a convert they went back to the car and drove to the next town. My friend told me, "They dropped me off at the nearest junction in the town centre. When I got out of the car I told the man, "If you think I would ever join such an evil group, you must be out of your mind. The power of Jesus is greater than any power."

And with that he ran off into the nearby crowd. The driver could not pursue him because there were too many people around.

God had saved my friend from certain death at the hands of ritual murderers. But God had tried to direct him through the umpire called peace. The uneasiness my friend had felt when he was getting into the car was a warning from God not to proceed.

In the ministry, you need to have peace about many things that you engage in. Sometimes there is no reason for peace. Sometimes you don't know why you are at peace. The Bible calls it "the peace that passes all understanding".

Chapter 11

How to Tell the Difference When the Spirit Speaks in Different Ways

The Voice of the Holy Spirit to Your Soul (Mind)

The Holy Spirit also speaks to our minds and directs us. What is it like when the Holy Spirit speaks to your mind? Anything that enters your mind is a thought. The Holy Spirit speaks to your mind by bringing thoughts to it.

But the Comforter, which is the Holy Ghost, whom the Father will send in my name, he shall teach you all things, and bring all things to your remembrance [mind], whatsoever I have said unto you.

John 14:26

This verse states clearly that the Holy Spirit will bring things to your mind. You must learn to distinguish between thoughts that come from your natural thought processes and thoughts that come from the Holy Spirit. There are also thoughts and suggestions that come from Satan.

Someone asked, "How do you know the voice of the Holy Spirit?" That is like asking, "How do I know the voice of my wife? Or for that matter anyone else?" By experience! The more I hear certain voices, the more easily I can identify them. Certain people call me on the telephone and do not need to introduce themselves. I know who they are when they begin to speak.

When you become conversant with the voice of the Holy Spirit to your spirit, soul or body, you will know when He speaks. I have many thoughts passing through my mind all the time. Just like everyone else, I have to filter these and decide which ones are natural and which ones are supernatural.

How I Heard That Voice in My Mind

Some years ago, I was dealing with a rebellious individual in my church. I felt strongly that this pastor was a rebel and that he was a liar. However, he had denied it on so many occasions that I doubted within myself whether this was the case. One day, while on a trip to Europe, the Holy Spirit spoke to my mind. I was lying down in bed when the Spirit of God spoke clearly into my mind. He said, "So-and-so is a liar and I will show you five different lies he has told you at different times."

Suddenly and in rapid succession, the Holy Spirit gave me five clear instances when this pastor had lied to me. They came so fast that I struggled to remember them afterwards. Then the Holy Spirit said, "Because of these, know that he is lying to you about this current problem." That was the turning point in my relationship with that particular minister. I suddenly knew that I was dealing with a prevaricator who by evasive and misleading answers had been able to live a lie.

God showed me that day that I had to deal with this rebellious and contumacious young man. And I did just that!

If you are a pastor, you will need the Spirit of God to lead you especially in relation to those who work with you. The spirit of Judas is the spirit of the perfect pretender. Sometimes you will never know of the deadly poison around you unless God reveals it to you supernaturally. I have found that the Spirit of God does these unusual things when there is no way for me to know certain things naturally! It is not the principal way that God speaks to you, but it is certainly an important method.

God speaks to your mind when He has to. The Bible makes it clear.

…[He will] bring all things to your remembrance [mind], whatsoever I have said unto you.

John 14:26

Many times when men of God say that God has spoken to them, they mean that certain thoughts came to their mind which they believe are from the Holy Spirit.

From today, have faith in the voice of the Holy Spirit speaking to your mind.

The Spirit of God says things to your mind (remembrance). When He speaks to your mind, you have distinctive, special and unique thoughts. It comes in a way that is unusual. It is learnt through experience and operated by faith.

The Voice of the Holy Spirit to Your Body

And as he journeyed, he came near Damascus: and suddenly there shined round about him a light from heaven: And he fell to the earth, and heard a voice saying unto him, Saul, Saul, why persecutest thou me? And he said, Who art thou, Lord? And the Lord said, I am Jesus whom thou persecutest: it is hard for thee to kick against the pricks.

Acts 9:3-5

You must also learn the voice of the Holy Spirit speaking to your physical being. *In this case, you will hear an audible voice speaking to you.* The Bible is full of such examples, however, do not make the mistake of thinking that it was an everyday occurrence with the Apostles.

Paul probably heard the voice of the Holy Spirit speaking to him in this way only once or twice in his lifetime. There is no need to seek these spectacular experiences. The devil knows when you have an appetite for sensational things. He is an expert at filling you with deception when he knows that you are vulnerable.

I have walked with the Lord for over twenty years. Once in my life, I believe I heard the audible voice of the Holy

Spirit speaking to me. But that is not the principal way by which the Holy Spirit leads me.

I believe I am called to the ministry. The proof of my call is in the fact that you are reading this book now! However, the Holy Spirit did not speak to me audibly to call me into the ministry. I have the quiet assurance of the voice of the Holy Spirit speaking to my heart. I know that I must be in the ministry. I know that I must not do anything else with my life. I must preach until I die. Like Paul said, "Woe is me if I preach not the Gospel." God does not need to give you a dramatic experience before you start obeying Him.

At different stages of my ministry, the Spirit has spoken to me in different ways. As far back as 1980, in Achimota Secondary School, I can remember the Spirit of God speaking to my spirit and giving me that inner knowing and peace about doing His work. Because of this, I have the conviction to serve God in the ministry as a pastor. It is this relaxed assurance that has put me in the ministry.

In 1988, in a remote village hospital of Ghana, the Spirit of God spoke to me audibly and showed me the direction to take in the ministry. In June 1996, in a small French village, the Spirit spoke to my mind and told me to start operating in certain areas of the ministry.

At each stage of my life the Holy Spirit has spoken to me in whatever way He found appropriate. He will also speak to you and you will get to know His voice as you walk with Him.

Chapter 12

Four Reasons for Spectacular Guidance

W e now come to more spectacular forms of guidance by the Holy Spirit. These include things like dreams, visions, trances, the appearance of angels and even the appearance of Jesus. We must ask ourselves why God chooses different methods each time. God is sovereign; He can decide to do whatever He wants.

I am not attempting to give a formula for how God speaks. I am just showing some patterns I have found in the Word of God. I would like to share with you four reasons why God may choose to speak to you in a spectacular way.

Four Reasons

1. God may speak in a spectacular way because it involves something very important for your life and ministry.

2. God may speak in a spectacular way because all other methods to reach you have not worked.

3. God may speak in a spectacular way because He sometimes shows mercy to stubborn people.

4. God may speak in a spectacular way because it involves something very important for His church.

Spectacular Guidance for Salvation

The Apostle Paul is an example of someone who experienced spectacular guidance. By the way, the fact that the guidance may not be spectacular does not mean it's not supernatural. Paul's salvation was not a typical case of conversion. I believe there are three reasons why God spoke to Paul in a spectacular way.

  a. Paul was destroying the church.

  Who was before...injurious:...

1 Timothy 1:13

  b. God wanted to show mercy to a stubborn person.

  Who was before a blasphemer,...

1 Timothy 1:13

  c.   God wanted to save Paul's life because no one can destroy the church and get away with it.

...it is hard for thee to kick against the pricks.

Acts 9:5

Spectacular Guidance for Joining the Right Church (Company)

Shortly after Paul's dramatic conversion, the Lord used another spectacular method to lead Paul into the right church so that he could have the right training for the ministry. Paul was a proud lawyer who might have thought that a few humble Jews could not teach him much.

...for one called Saul, of Tarsus: for, behold, he prayeth, And hath seen in a vision a man named Ananias coming in, and putting his hand on him, that he might receive his sight.

Acts 9:11,12

The visions surrounding Paul's direction to join the main church were so dramatic that Paul couldn't help but listen to the counsel of older and more experienced Christians. I believe that God did this because it involved the future ministry to the entire "Gentile" world.

Spectacular Guidance for Where to Start a Church

One day Paul made plans to travel to Bithynia. He wanted to start a ministry there, but the Spirit of God had other plans. That night the Spirit of God spoke to Paul in a vision. He saw a man standing in Macedonia and saying, "Come over into Mecedonia, and help us." Once again, this was very important for the building of the church.

Spectacular Guidance for Survival

Further on in Paul's ministry a situation arose which threatened his very life. He was about to die in a shipwreck (plane crash). An angel suddenly appeared and told him what to do.

> **But after long abstinence Paul stood forth in the midst of them, and said, Sirs, ye should have hearkened unto me, and not have loosed from Crete, and to have gained this harm and loss. And now I exhort you to be of good cheer: for there shall be no loss of any man's life among you, but of the ship. For there stood by me this night the angel of God, whose I am, and whom I serve, Saying, Fear not, Paul; thou must be brought before Caesar: and, lo, God hath given thee all them that sail with thee. Wherefore, sirs, be of good cheer: for I believe God, that it shall be even as it was told me.**
>
> **Acts 27:21-25**

Because of the angelic visitation, Paul directed everyone to eat some food. This saved their lives and enabled them to survive until they ran aground.

As you can see, one or more of the four reasons given at the beginning of this chapter is always present when God speaks in a spectacular way.

Spectacular Guidance to Help You Endure a Difficult Season

Paul was going to go through a very difficult period as a prisoner. He was about to be arrested and kept in prison cells until he died. This was an important part of Paul's ministry because it was there that he wrote many of his letters. It is by these letters that Paul's ministry has lived on for two thousand years.

And as we tarried there many days, there came down from Judaea a certain prophet, named Agabus. And when he was come unto us, he took Paul's girdle, and bound his own hands and feet, and said, Thus saith the Holy Ghost, So shall the Jews at Jerusalem bind the man that owneth this girdle, and shall deliver him into the hands of the Gentiles.

Acts 21:10,11

Chapter 13

How to Identify a Door

...Behold, I have set before thee an OPEN DOOR,...

Revelation 3:8

1. An open door is a *God-given opportunity* in the midst of impossibilities.

2. An open door is a *chance to escape or to achieve something* for the Lord.

3. An open door is an *opening in the midst of impassable circustances*.

4. An open door is a *time-related breakthrough* that gives you a needed option.

Three Ways to Recognize a Door

1.   **The first way to recognize a door is to recognize an opportunity that comes in the midst of other unworkable options.**

In the natural, a door is flanked on the left and right by impenetrable walls. This reveals impossible or impenetrable circumstances all around except in the position where the door is.

...I will tarry at Ephesus... For A GREAT DOOR and effectual is opened...

1 Corinthians 16:8,9

Paul decided to remain at Ephesus because of the opportunities to minister over there. All around him were hostile cities that were not open to the Gospel. **When you are *flanked* by impossibilities and one niche opens up, it is often God opening a door for you.**

2.   **The second way to recognize a door is to discern that it is an opportunity that will not always be there.**

In the natural, a door does not have a fixed position. It is either open or closed. Any opportunity that appears for a season and disappears again must be considered as a door.

...I will tarry at Ephesus...For A GREAT DOOR and effectual is OPENED...

1 Corinthians 16:8,9

Even though there was an opportunity for ministry at Ephesus, that opportunity would not be there forever. Today, there is very little opportunity for ministry in Ephesus. The door is shut in many parts of Europe. However, the door is now open in many parts of Africa and the developing world. These doors will not remain open forever. Instability and war may close them one day. It is our duty to go through the doors when they swing open. When the "Iron Curtain" came down, there was a sudden open door for the Gospel in Eastern Europe. This door is gradually closing again.

3.   **The third way to recognize a door is to realize that God engineered the opportunity and that it had nothing to do with your efforts.**

In the natural, you do not often construct the doors you meet. Everyone just passes through the doors that are open. An open door is not of your own making, it is just something that you benefit from.

And when they were come, and had gathered the church together, they rehearsed all that God had done with them, and how *HE* HAD OPENED THE DOOR of faith unto the Gentiles.

Acts 14:27

When Paul and Barnabas gave the report of their first missionary journey, everyone was overjoyed at what the Lord had done. They came to one conclusion: God had opened a door to the Gentiles! They knew that only God could do it! That is how to recognize a door. Recognize that it is only God who could have made that opportunity possible.

Chapter 14

How to Recognize a Door of Service

There are some important doors that every Christian must recognize and pass through. God often uses doors to direct His children.

The Door of Service

But I will tarry at Ephesus until Pentecost. For A GREAT DOOR AND EFFECTUAL is opened unto me, and there are many adversaries.

1 Corinthians 16:8,9

The door of service is the opportunity to be effective for the Lord. The door of service is the opportunity to serve the Lord. We cannot effectively win souls for Jesus all the time. A time comes when it is not possible anymore. Sometimes marriage, pregnancy and childbearing close the door of service. If you grasp the opportunity whilst it is there, you will experience many blessings. When you follow the door of service, you gain two important qualifications. These are:

a. You graduate from being a novice.

God does not put inexperienced people into the ministry. You need experience to be effective as a minister. *What have you been through? What have you survived? What have you suffered?*

Not a novice, lest being lifted up with pride he fall into the condemnation of the devil.

1 Timothy 3:6

b. You prove yourself so that you can be put into an office.

There are four levels in the line of God's service.

Level one – doing the work. "...do the work of an evangelist..." (2 Timothy 4:5).

Level two – having a gift. "Having then gifts differing..." (Romans 12:6)

Level three – having a ministry. "...make full proof of thy ministry" (2 Timothy 4:5).

Level four – occupying an office. "...I magnify mine office" (Romans 11:13).

Take the evangelistic line of ministry. You could do the work of an evangelist, but that does not mean that you are in the *office* of an evangelist. Like Timothy, you may be temporarily getting involved in the *work* of evangelism. At the next level, you could have a *gift* of evangelism. That does not mean that you are in the ministry of an evangelist, but with an additional step, you could progress into the *ministry* of an evangelist. At this point, it has become your permanent line of service.

At the highest level, you could actually be in the *office* of an evangelist. When you occupy an office, you are at the highest level in that line of ministry. When you are at the office level, you need to employ people to assist you. When there are several people helping and serving under you in your line of ministry, it is often a sign that you are occupying a spiritual *office*.

> **And let these also first be proved; then let them use the office of a deacon, being found blameless.**
>
> **1 Timothy 3:10**

The door of service will show that you are faithful in little things. Then you can be trusted with greater things.

> **He that is faithful in that which is least is faithful also in much:...**
>
> **Luke 16:10**

As you follow the doors of service, you will often find yourself doing menial jobs in the ministry. You may be in the background. You may not be seen or praised for what you do, but do not be worried, your reward is guaranteed. The reward for those who went and those who stayed behind is the same. This is a law that was established by King David.

> **...but as his part is that GOETH down to the battle, so shall his part be that TARRIETH by the stuff: THEY SHALL PART ALIKE.**
>
> **1 Samuel 30:24**

Chapter 15

How to Recognize a Door of Utterance

Withal praying also for us, that God would open unto us a door of utterance, to speak the mystery of Christ...

Colossians 4:3

The Door of Utterance

A door of utterance is an opportunity to preach or teach. Every opportunity to share the Word must be seized. It is a God-given chance to minister. Any time you share the Word you become more mature. Did you know that the preacher is the one who is most affected by the sermon?

The more you preach, the better you become at ministry. A door of utterance is a door of excellence for you.

Chapter 16

How to Recognize a Door of Faith

And when they were come, and had gathered the church together, they rehearsed all that God had done with them, and how he had opened the door of faith unto the Gentiles.

Acts 14:27

The Door of Faith

A door of faith is the opportunity for salvation for someone. As you relate with people you must discern whether a door of faith is being opened. In Europe for instance, the door of faith (salvation) is shut. This does not mean that people cannot be saved in Europe. But the opportunity for salvation is much greater in some other places.

Sometimes someone goes through a personal crisis and becomes more open to the message of Christ. A door of faith is being opened unto that person. Seize the opportunity and minister the Gospel to him.

Chapter 17

What Every Christian Should Know About Dreams

All of us have had dreams from the time that we were very young. Dreams are so common that many Christians have grown up not respecting dreams as a valid method by which God leads us. We seem to think that after all, we had all kinds of dreams as children and also as unbelievers, and we wonder how God can lead us through dreams.

Dreams from the Holy Spirit

Surprisingly, God's Word teaches us that the coming of the Holy Spirit will bring dreams into our lives.

And it shall come to pass in the last days, saith God, I will pour out of my Spirit upon all flesh: and your sons and your daughters shall prophesy, and your young men shall see visions, and your old men shall dream dreams:

Acts 2:17

You can see from this Scripture that dreams come as a direct result of the presence of the Holy Spirit. From today, do not take dreams lightly! This however, does not discount the fact that dreams can come from sources other than the Holy Spirit.

We will examine this also, but what must be established in your heart is the reality that many dreams are the result of the presence of the Holy Spirit. In the book of Job, God reveals that He speaks in dreams when He cannot get our attention. An unusual dream is always something that gets our attention.

For God speaketh once, yea twice, yet man perceiveth it not.

Job 33:14

There are times when God may speak to us, but we don't seem to hear. The Bible goes on to say,

IN A DREAM, in a vision of the night, when deep sleep falleth upon men, in slumberings upon the bed; THEN HE OPENETH THE EARS OF MEN, and sealeth their instruction,

Job 33:15,16

Sometimes you wake up in the morning with an unusual dream. It may be that God is trying to get your attention. From today, do not despise dreams. If you consider the birth of Jesus, you will discover how dreams played an important role in the life of Joseph and Mary.

It was a dream that led Joseph to marry Mary, in spite of the fact that she was found to be pregnant before they were married.

> **But while he thought on these things, behold, the angel of the Lord appeared unto him in a dream, saying, Joseph, thou son of David, fear not to take unto thee Mary thy wife: for that which is conceived in her is of the Holy Ghost. And she shall bring forth a son, and thou shalt call his name JESUS: for he shall save his people from their sins.**

Matthew 1:20,21

It was through a dream that Joseph was directed to flee into Egypt for the safety of the baby Jesus. Because Joseph obeyed this dream, Jesus escaped the slaughter of babies that was ordered by Herod.

> **And when they were departed, behold, the angel of the Lord appeareth to Joseph in a dream, saying, Arise, and take the young child and his mother, and flee into Egypt, and be thou there until I bring thee word: for Herod will seek the young child to destroy him.**

Matthew 2:13

When Herod died, God spoke yet again by a dream and asked Joseph to return to the land of Israel.

> **But when Herod was dead, behold, AN ANGEL OF THE LORD APPEARETH IN A DREAM TO JOSEPH in Egypt, Saying, Arise, and take the young child and his mother, and go into the land of Israel: for they are dead which sought the young child's life.**

> **Matthew 2:19,20**

Joseph was directed yet again to move away from Judea into Galilee and into a city called Nazareth. Because of this, Jesus was called a Nazarene.

> **...being warned of God in a dream, he turned aside into the parts of Galilee: And he came and dwelt in a city called Nazareth:...**

> **Matthew 2:22,23**

Joseph had *four* dreams in all. By following the direction that he received in each dream, the perfect will of God was done. Prophecies were fulfilled and the Scriptures were confirmed because a man obeyed a dream.

The Apostle Paul was careful to take note of important dreams and visions. He stated that he did not disobey heavenly visions.

> **Whereupon, O king Agrippa, I was NOT DISOBEDIENT UNTO THE HEAVENLY VISION:**

> **Acts 26:19**

Paul was someone who respected the voice of God that came to him. It is important for you to accept the fact that God does speak to us through dreams. A "vision in the night" is another biblical description for a dream.

And a vision appeared to Paul in the night; There stood a man of Macedonia, and prayed him, saying, Come over into Macedonia, and help us. And after he had seen the vision, immediately we endeavoured to go into Macedonia, assuredly gathering that the Lord had called us for to preach the gospel unto them.

Acts 16:9,10

From this Scripture, notice how Paul became assured of what to do. One of the ways by which the Holy Spirit leads us is through a dream.

Apostle Peter had an important dream that changed the course of his ministry. Peter was praying on the rooftop while the ladies prepared food downstairs. Whilst praying, he fell into a trance and had a quick dream. In this dream he saw many strange animals and heard a voice saying, "Rise, Peter; kill and eat."

On the morrow, as they went on their journey, and drew nigh unto the city, Peter went up upon the housetop to pray about the sixth hour: And he became very hungry, and would have eaten: but while they made ready, he fell into a trance, And saw heaven opened, and a certain vessel descending unto him, as it had been a great sheet knit at the four corners, and let down to the earth: Wherein were all manner of fourfooted beasts of the earth, and wild beasts, and creeping things, and fowls of the air. And there came a voice to him, Rise, Peter; kill, and eat. But Peter said, Not so, Lord; for I have never eaten any thing that is common or unclean. And the voice spake unto him again the second time, What God

hath cleansed, that call not thou common. This was done thrice: and the vessel was received up again into heaven.

Acts 10:9-16

This trance or short dream that Peter had, was an important instruction from God to the head of His church. God was telling Peter to go and minister to the Gentiles.

There are times when, just like Peter, you may fall asleep while you are praying. Always take note of the dreams you have at such times. They may be Spirit-inspired messages from the Lord.

Chapter 18

How to Interpret Different Kinds of Dreams

The problem with dreams is that there are four different types of dreams and that can confuse us. Sometimes, because of multiple meaningless dreams, many mature Christians tend to totally ignore the importance of dreams. The four types of dreams are:

i.   Dreams from the Holy Spirit

ii.   Dreams from your daily activities

iii.   Dreams from the flesh

iv.   Dreams from the devil

Dreams from Your Daily Activities

These are dreams that emanate from your everyday activities. The Bible teaches us that a dream comes as a result of our activities or businesses.

For a dream cometh through the multitude of business;...

Ecclesiastes 5:3

Maybe you were out the entire day with a certain Christian gentleman. A few days later or perhaps that very evening, you have a dream that you were getting married to him. Although this dream could have come from the Holy Spirit, it is more likely that it came as a result of your interaction with him.

Whenever you have a dream, check to see if there is any relationship between your dream and what is going on in your life. It does not have to be something that has happened in your life that very day. It sometimes takes a few weeks before your business activities give rise to a dream.

You must be careful not to say a dream comes from the Holy Spirit when it has come from your own activities. In addition to this, a dream from God must be taken in context with the other ways in which the Holy Spirit speaks.

If the Holy Spirit is speaking to you in a dream, ask yourself whether it lines up with the peace of God in your heart (peace the umpire).

Dreams from the Flesh

One of the common dreams that people experience is having sexual intercourse with another person. Many times those who have such dreams interpret it to mean that they are "spiritually married" to somebody else. However, these dreams are often a night-time continuation of fleshly lusts.

Often the individual involved has experienced several sexual encounters with people. Such dreams sometimes reveal the state of our minds and hearts.

Likewise also these FILTHY DREAMERS DEFILE THE FLESH, despise dominion, and speak evil of dignities.

Jude 8

There is something known as a filthy dream and there are people who are filthy dreamers. These people defile the flesh. In other words, they make it dirty. It is time to stop placing the blame on a "marinespirit" or a curse. It is time to face up to the reality that filthy dreams come from a carnal nature that has been allowed to have its way time and time again.

Paul said that he controlled his flesh. Paul had a carnal nature that had a tendency to go out of control. If you allow your mind and your flesh to do anything, it will! The Bible teaches us that there is no good thing in the flesh.

For I know that in me (that is, in my flesh,) dwelleth no good thing:...

Romans 7:18

There is no good thing in your fleshly nature. Do not give it an opportunity to go out of bounds.

...make not provision for the flesh, to fulfil the lusts thereof.

Romans 13:14

77

Dreams from the Devil

As usual, the devil has a counterfeit for everything that God does. Satan's specialty is to deceive and to trick.

God is not the author of confusion. **A dream, which brings confusion, is not from God.** The Spirit of God is not a spirit of fear. Something that comes to frighten you is not from the Spirit of the Lord.

Many people have been snared by the devil through dreams. Satan will give you a picture of some evil event and tell you that the dream is going to happen. The devil may show you a picture of your coffin and your funeral. Many Christians have been trapped into disasters, untimely deaths and all manner of wickedness by demonic dreams.

How People are Trapped by Demonic Dreams

People are trapped into childlessness and barrenness by means of dreams. This is how it happens: Satan shows them a picture of barrenness or a picture of them sleeping with someone else. These dreams have one aim; to frighten you and to instil fear into your heart.

Then thou SCAREST me with dreams, and TERRIFIEST me through visions:

Job 7:14

You begin to fear that you will not have a child. You begin to fear that things will not work out normally for you. After all, your dreams show you unknown people sleeping with you! When fear has taken a foothold, the real thing can happen! Fear is not a mood or a feeling; it is a demonic spirit.

For God hath not given us the *SPIRIT* OF FEAR;...

2 Timothy 1:7

Remember that Job eventually experienced what he was afraid of. God had blessed him. God had given him houses, lands, prosperity, children and great riches. Yet, he was afraid that something bad could happen to him. Eventually, his fears came to pass.

For the thing which I greatly feared is come upon me, and that which I was afraid of is come unto me.

Job 3:25

Be careful of the things that you fear because the things that you fear will happen! That is why Jesus often said, "FEAR NOT! Only believe!"

Many years ago, when I was living with my parents, thieves invaded our home. I happened to wake up in the night at about 3:00 a.m. and I heard some noise downstairs. A gang of thieves had broken into our house and were carrying away everything that they could. I shouted, waking up the entire neighbourhood, but the thieves escaped in a get-away car!

Later on, I discovered how the thieves were able to get into the house. They had removed two louvre blades from the window and helped one of their gang members to enter the house. It must have been a very small individual because the space created was very small. **This person who entered the house then opened the main doors and let the rest of the robbers (demons) in.**

This is how the devil works. He just needs to get one member of his team into your mind. That one spirit will open the door for many other demons to enter.

When fear is allowed to take a foothold in your life, it opens the door to destruction, untimely death, sickness and barrenness. Job said that he was frightened by dreams. God will not send you a spirit of fear. Later on when these frightening dreams occur people say, "You see, it has happened just as I dreamt." **No! It has happened just as you feared!**

Chapter 19

How to Relate to a Prophet

There are many people who feel that they must be led by a personal prophecy coming from a prophet. I personally know of many Christians who have made major changes in their lives because of something a prophet told them. Is this scriptural?

In this chapter, I want to share with you about what I believe is the proper role of a prophet in the Church. You must know what a prophet is supposed to do, otherwise, you may find your life destroyed by someone claiming to be a prophet.

...O my people, they which lead thee cause thee to err, and destroy the way of thy paths.

Isaiah 3:12

Are our lives supposed to be guided by prophets? The answer is NO! As New Testament believers we are supposed to be guided by the Holy Spirit and the Word of God.

For as many as are led by the Spirit of God, they are the sons of God.

Romans 8:14

The role that the prophets of the Old Testament played was different from that of New Testament prophets. Am I saying that New Testament prophets did not have the power to see visions and receive "words" from the Lord? They certainly did have this power but it operated within a different context.

Under the Old Covenant, only the prophet and perhaps the priest had the Holy Spirit working through them. Today, the Holy Spirit is in every believer and is giving us personal guidance on a day-to-day basis. **We still need the input of prophets, but we do not need to seek them for daily guidance.** We also need to check whatever they say, to see whether it agrees with what the Holy Spirit is telling us.

Let the prophets speak two or three, and let the other judge.

1 Corinthians 14:29

Under the New Testament, the declarations of prophets are supposed to be judged or assessed. How can we judge what the prophet says if we don't have the Holy Spirit or the Word? The Word of God provides a standard by which we can assess what is happening.

For instance, I have noticed how many prophets minister in churches, giving personal prophecies to individuals. I have watched prophets telling members of one particular church that the Lord wants them to move out of that church into the church that he, the prophet, is establishing.

There are prophets who have destabilized entire churches with this type of message. I know a church that lost about five hundred members through the ministry of one such prophet. This same visiting prophet gave a prophecy to the associate pastor of the church, telling him that the Lord wanted him to move on. The next thing we discovered was that this associate pastor had become a resident pastor in the prophet's new church.

If I were to judge such an action by the Word of God, I would quote to you from the book of Ephesians. Paul shows us the role of apostles, prophets, evangelists, pastors and teachers. They are to minister to the Body of Christ so that the saints become stable Christians. Read it for yourself:

And he gave some, apostles; and some, prophets,...That we henceforth be no more children, tossed to and fro, and carried about...

Ephesians 4:11,14

If a true prophet comes to minister in your church, you will know him by his fruits. If the fruit (the end result) of his ministry were destabilization and a moving of church members to and fro, I would wonder whether he's a New Testament prophet. Read it for yourself! Prophets are supposed to minister and prevent the to and fro movement of church members. They are supposed to prevent them from being carried about by every new idea.

I would not advise any pastor to welcome a so-called prophet to destabilize the church that he has taken years to build. As a pastor, my duty is to gather sheep. My call is to prevent them from being lost. **I want to be able to say to**

Jesus, **"Of all that you have given me, I have lost none."** I believe that I am a good pastor so I will fight for every single sheep that God has assigned to me.

The Reaping Prophet

I remember having a discussion with a certain prophet. This prophet had ministered privately to several prominent church members of mine, telling them that the Lord wanted them to move out of my church. The prophet did not know that I knew about these different destabilizing "prophecies" he had given to my people. In fact, as at the time we were speaking, some of my church members had become members of his church.

I asked him, "How is the ministry?"

He said, "It's doing well. I have had a few problems but I am surviving."

We got to discuss other things. Then he told me, "You know, I invited a prophet to minister in my church." (Although he was a prophet, he was pastoring a church.)

He continued, "This prophet really did me in."

"What do you mean?" I asked.

"I invited him to minister in my church and he began to prophesy to all my members and directed them to see him privately," he explained.

He lamented, "By the time this prophet had finished the convention, I had lost a large section of my church to him. This prophet gave accurate prophecies, and after the faith of the people was lifted, he told them that God wanted them to leave their church."

I listened quietly as the prophet/pastor spoke of his experience.

"He has met his match," I thought to myself, "Perhaps he has forgotten similar prophecies which he gave to my church members!"

This prophet did not know that he was reaping the destabilization he had sown in other people's churches.

You do not need a prophet to tell you which church to attend. You do not need a prophet to tell you whom to marry. You do not need a prophet to tell you to give away your car or your life's savings. You have the *Word of God*! You have the *Holy Spirit* and you have your *common sense* that we spoke about in an earlier chapter.

The Bible tells us that God speaks to us in the New Testament, mainly by His Word and not by His prophets.

God, who at sundry times and in divers manners spake in time past unto the fathers by the prophets, Hath in these last days spoken unto us by his Son [the Word]...

Hebrews 1:1,2

Do not allow any so-called prophet to rob you of your possessions. The accuracy of prophecies can be so frightening that you will feel that God must be speaking. Sometimes, some prophets have an evil spirit operating through them. They give accurate "words of knowledge" by satanic power and then they rob you of your money.

There are also some prophets who operate by a mixture of spirits. They will minister very accurately by the Spirit of God. After realizing how enchanted you are by the accuracy of the gift, they will move into the flesh and operate by another spirit. Is it possible for someone to operate with two different spirits at the same time? Of course it is! Samson had the Spirit of God operating in him, whilst at the same time he was operating in a spirit of adultery and fornication.

Remember when Jesus asked Peter, "Who do men say that I am?" Peter answered accurately. Jesus immediately confirmed that Peter was moving in the Holy Spirit. There was no way Peter could have known what he knew, except the Spirit of God had revealed it to him. However, in the discussion that followed, Peter began to speak as inspired by Satan and Jesus had to rebuke him saying, "Satan, get thee behind me." Watch Peter under the influence of the Holy Spirit.

He saith unto them, But whom say ye that I am? And Simon Peter answered and said, Thou art the Christ, the Son of the living God. And Jesus answered and said unto him, Blessed art thou, Simon Barjona: for FLESH AND BLOOD HATH NOT REVEALED IT UNTO THEE, BUT MY FATHER WHICH IS IN HEAVEN.

Matthew 16:15-17

Now watch Peter under the influence of Satan.

From that time forth began Jesus to shew unto his disciples, how that he must go unto Jerusalem, and suffer many things of the elders and chief priests and scribes, and be killed, and be raised again the third day. Then Peter took him, and began to rebuke him, saying, Be it far from thee, Lord: this shall not be unto thee. But he turned, and said unto Peter, Get thee behind me, Satan: THOU ART AN OFFENSE UNTO ME: for thou savourest not the things that be of God, but those that be of men.

Matthew 16:21-23

How to Relate with a Real Prophet

So what exactly is a prophet supposed to do? How should I relate to someone who calls himself a prophet? Let us study the ministry of Jesus since He was a great prophet. Each office of the Body of Christ: apostle, prophet, evangelist, pastor and teacher, has several different ministries under it. A prophet will also have different ministries operating under his office.

A minister who stands in the office of a prophet will primarily function in the ministry of preaching and teaching. Beware of so-called prophets who do not preach the Word of God but only give personal prophecies. Don't misunderstand me, I believe in personal prophecies.

However, let it be very clear that anything that does not put the Word of God in its proper place is doomed to failure with the passage of time. "In the beginning was the *Word*..." "Let the *Word* of Christ dwell in you richly..." "Thy *Word* is a light unto my path... The entrance of thy *Word* giveth light..." Anything without the *Word* is in darkness and is not of God.

All offices of the ministry have a primary function of teaching and preaching. The Word comes first and is of paramount importance in every ministerial office. After preaching and teaching the Word, a prophet may operate in the ministry of healing, and other revelation gifts like the "word of knowledge" and "word of wisdom". The prophet may also flow in the ministry of predictive prophecy or exhortative prophecy. From Scripture, you will see that Jesus was a great prophet.

...and they glorified God, saying, That a great prophet is risen up among us;...

Luke 7:16

But His principal ministry was to go about preaching and teaching the Word of God.

And Jesus went about all the cities and villages, teaching in their synagogues, and preaching the gospel...

Matthew 9:35

Jesus had a healing ministry.

How God anointed Jesus...who went about doing good, and healing all that were oppressed of the devil;...

Acts 10:38

He also operated in the gifts of revelation. Standing in the office of a prophet, He ministered to the woman of Samaria;

For thou hast had five husbands; and he whom thou now hast is not thy husband:...

John 4:18

The woman of Samaria immediately realized that she had met someone standing in the office of a prophet. Look at her response to Jesus' ministration.

The woman saith unto him, Sir, I perceive that thou art a prophet.

John 4:19

Jesus also operated in the ministry of predictive prophecy. In the book of Matthew, Chapter 24, He predicted the destruction of Solomon's temple. This happened in 70 AD when the Romans destroyed Jerusalem.

Speaking of the temple He said,

...There shall not be left here one stone upon another,...

Matthew 24:2

Jesus gave extensive predictions concerning the end of the world. We would do well to take note of these prophecies because Jesus was a great prophet.

The Ministry of a Prophet

It is clear from the above account that a prophet is someone who *preaches* and *teaches*. He also ministers *healing* and operates in the word of *knowledge*. A prophet also gives predictive and exhortative *prophesies*. This is a complete prophetic ministry, and as you can see, the Word of God comes first. Look out for real prophets and stay with what is authentic. Look for proven prophets whose foundation is the Word of God. That is how to relate to your prophet.

Chapter 20

How to Use the Word of God for Direction

The Bible contains the written Word of God. It is a reliable source of direction for us all. The Word of God is a silent voice. How can a voice be silent? The silent voices are a group of voices that the Holy Spirit uses to guide us. They are silent in the sense that you do not hear a person speaking audibly. They are however, common ways by which the Holy Spirit leads us all. You see, being led by the Spirit of God is not a very simple thing. Today, human beings communicate by speech, by touch, by facial expressions, by letters, faxes, telephones, television, e-mail and so on. There are also many methods by which God communicates with His children. One of these is the written Word of God.

The Word of God

The Word of God is given to us for direction in our lives. Everything we do must be done according to the Word of God. In a very general way, the Word of God is the perfect guidebook for our lives. The Bible is a unique book that contains instruction on every possible issue that may arise. There are many people who think that the Bible is not a practical and relevant book for today.

One lady told me that she believed she could practise fornication because the Bible was out of fashion. Three years later, when her boyfriend of many years ditched her, she realized that the Bible was not so archaic after all.

All scripture is given by inspiration of God, and is profitable for doctrine, for reproof, for correction, for instruction in righteousness: That the man of God may be perfect, throughly furnished unto all good works.

2 Timothy 3:16,17

The scripture is profitable, useful, relevant and practical for every Christian today! There are many Christians who do not want you to open the Bible; they just want a prophecy or a word of knowledge.

The Word Is a Light

...I have ordained a lamp for mine anointed.

Psalm 132:17

The Art of Hearing

Use the Word of God as a light for your path. There is so much darkness in the world. We often do not know what to do, but God has provided a light for Christians. What is this light that God has provided for Christians?

Thy word is a lamp unto my feet, and a light unto my path.

Psalm 119:105

God's Word is a lamp and a light for us. It is only when you put on the light that you know where to go. It is only when you put on the light that you can prevent yourself from stumbling over furniture. Jesus Christ called Himself the light of this world.

...I am the light of the world: he that followeth me shall not walk in darkness, but shall have the light of life.

John 8:12

You need light in this life! Jesus (the Word) is the light for your life. People who have tried to live their lives without Christ and the Word have discovered that it is painful to stumble around in the darkness.

A young man approached me and informed me that he was having terrible problems in his marriage. He wanted me to help him. He wanted to know the way out of his marital difficulties. As I talked with him, I realized that what he needed was the Word. He said to me, "Are you going to pray for me to have my deliverance?"

I asked, "Why do you need deliverance?"

He answered, "Oh, I was told that my wife has a marine spirit."

I asked him, "What is a marine spirit?"

He said, "Oh, it's something they say I have to be delivered from. So I want you to deliver me." I thought to myself, "This man wants a quick fix. He does not want the Word. He does not know that nothing sets you free like the Word of God does."

And ye shall know the truth, and the truth shall make you free.

John 8:32

I asked him, "Are you a born-again Christian?"

"Yes, I am."

"Are you faithful to your wife?" I asked.

He smiled, "Um… not really."

"Actually", he continued, "I have not been faithful to her at all!"

I advised this man to have a pastor and belong to a church. I told him, "Your marine spirit is the least of your problems. What you need is the Word of God to guide you in this life. **You need the light of life, otherwise, you will continue to grope in darkness.**"

There are people who wonder how I know the things I do. I remember arriving in Johannesburg one day for a convention. I was met by a South African delegation. When they saw me, one of them asked, "Are you the Bishop?"

I said, "Yes, I am."

"Really! We were expecting someone much older! We have listened to your tapes and read your books. Somehow, we thought you were a much older person." When you walk in the Word, people will think you are much older than your real age.

The Word Is Wisdom

Thou through thy commandments hast made me wiser than mine enemies:...I have more understanding than all my teachers: for thy testimonies are my meditation.

Psalm 119:98,99

The Word of God will make you wise in this life. Advice and direction for business are found in the Word of God. There is more instruction for a businessperson in the Word of God than in any lecture on business management. There is more relevant and practical knowledge on philosophy, political science, literature and history in the Bible than in any other book I know.

The Word Is Instruction

I sometimes smile when people say, "God has called me to do such-and-such for Him." If you do not obey the simple instructions in the Word, do you think God is going to give you more? He that is faithful in little is faithful in much. If you do not obey the Word of God which says to pay your tithes, do you think God is going to speak to you about a miracle healing ministry?

He hath shewed thee, O man, what is good; and what doth the LORD require of thee,...

Micah 6:8

God will minister His Word to you through pastors and shepherds. That is why it is important to have a good church and a pastor who teaches the Word of God. Whenever your pastor is preaching, be open to receive direction for your life.

The Word Brings Understanding

In the last days, God is giving pastors who will feed us with knowledge and understanding. Receive the knowledge and understanding that God is giving you.

And I will give you pastors according to mine heart, which shall feed you with knowledge and understanding.

Jeremiah 3:15

God will also use men of God to give you instructions for your life. These instructions help you to become a better person. There are times your pastor will give a commandment to fast and pray. It is important to follow these instructions. The Bible teaches that we should obey those that have spiritual authority over us.

Obey them that have the rule over you, and submit yourselves: for they watch for your souls...

Hebrews 13:17

Listen to the voice of your shepherd. God has delegated the destiny of the sheep to the shepherd. God will bless your life and lead you through the voice of your shepherd. Jesus is the overall shepherd and He told Peter to look after the sheep. That means that He was delegating the care of His sheep to under-shepherds.

...Simon, son of Jonas, lovest thou me?....Jesus saith unto him, Feed my sheep.

John 21:17

Chapter 21

The Secret of Directed Paths

Trust in the LORD with all thine heart; and lean not unto thine own understanding. In all thy ways acknowledge him, and he shall direct thy paths.

Proverbs 3:5,6

God leads us through directed paths. The promise of God in this Scripture is not that God will direct you! God is promising here that He will direct your paths. What is the difference between God directing you and God directing your paths? When God directs you, He speaks to you and tells you what to do. It is then up to you to do the right thing and obey His voice. However, when God directs your paths, you don't have to do anything. It is your paths that have to obey instructions.

Your duty is to trust the Lord that He has arranged the circumstances so that you will naturally flow into His will. This is what happens when you pray, "Thy will be done." Jesus prayed "Thy will be done" for three hours in the Garden of Gethsemane. After getting an answer to that prayer, Jesus didn't have to do anything any more. He just allowed things to happen naturally.

God Ignores You and Speaks to Your Paths

Once I was walking in a major international airport. Those of you who have travelled a bit know that modern airports are monstrous buildings with an often intricate maze of tunnels and corridors. This was the first time I had been in that particular airport. I travel frequently so I know my way around many major airports. This time however, I did not know the way. When I got out of the plane I just kept walking. As I walked in that airport, God gave me a revelation.

I didn't get lost at all, not even for one minute! I walked confidently through the labyrinth of airport corridors and arrived at the right place to pick up my baggage. Would you believe that no one told me where to go or what to do, but I just kept walking?

God showed me that I did not get lost in that airport because the authorities had arranged the corridors and tunnels in such a way that I could only go in one direction and arrive in one particular place.

As I walked through the airport, I realized that many doors were shut. Access to many parts of the airport was blocked to me. There were signs everywhere showing where newly arrived passengers should go.

That is often how God will lead you if you will take the time to pray that His will be done in your life. Then you can walk on confidently. **You may not even know what exactly to do, but as you keep on praying that His will be done, He will direct your paths.** God will block certain doors and make it impossible for you to go on certain roads.

He will ensure that you will only flow in a particular direction. He will ensure that you only meet certain people.

There are many times I don't know what to do. I am not a superman. I cannot pretend to know the mind of God all the time. Nobody knows all the will of God. Even Jesus prayed that the will of God be done. I spend hours praying that the will of God be done in my life. I believe that every serious Christian should do that!

If you have committed your way to God, as the Bible says in Proverbs 3:5 and 6, God is committed to directing the paths of your life.

Do not cry any more because that man did not marry you. Do not be sad because that opportunity did not work out. Did you not pray that the will of God should be done? Did you not commit your ways to Him? God is answering your prayers right now! He is directing your life. You do not have to hear a voice. You do not need to see a vision. **Just continue walking by faith and you will find yourself in His perfect will.**

Chapter 22

How to Deal with the Voice of the People

Another important area of influence is the voice of human beings. What others say and do influence many people. Most of the time we want to be like others. Whatever the people in your peer group are doing is what you want to do! But many times that is not the will of God.

God created a special nation called Israel. He planned to rule the nation directly through His prophets and spiritual leaders. When the people of Israel realized that all the nations around them had kings, they also decided to have a king. Even though what they were experiencing was better, they just wanted to follow the crowd.

The voice of the people and their voice of God are mutually exclusive, one must cancel out the other.

**Then all the elders of Israel gathered themselves
together, and came to Samuel unto Ramah, And said
unto him, Behold, thou art old, and thy sons walk
not in thy ways: NOW MAKE US A KING TO
JUDGE US LIKE ALL THE NATIONS. And the
LORD said unto Samuel, Hearken unto the voice of
the people in all that they say unto thee: for they
have not rejected thee, but they have rejected me,
that I should not reign over them...howbeit yet
protest solemnly unto them,...Nevertheless the
people refused to obey the voice of Samuel; and they
said, NAY; BUT WE WILL HAVE A KING OVER
US; THAT WE ALSO MAY BE LIKE ALL THE
NATIONS;...**

1 Samuel 8:4,5,7,9,19,20

That is what I call "the voice of the people". It is such a
strong voice that it often drowns out the gentle voice of the
Holy Spirit. You must be careful not to become someone who
is easily affected by the opinions of those around. No one can
be a successful minister if he still wants to please people
around. That is why a church must not be run by democracy.
The essential nature of democracy turns people into men-
pleasers and liars.

**...for if I yet pleased men, I should not be the servant
of Christ.**

Galatians 1:10

If you want to serve the Lord, you must be careful not to
become a man-pleaser. I am wary of people who are very
conscious of making good impressions everywhere. Such
people are usually two-faced and can easily betray you.

On the 10th of March 1989, I qualified as a medical doctor. I was pastoring this fledgling church along with some other medical colleagues of mine. As was the custom, after one year of working in the hospital, most of my colleagues left the country for the USA and England. They were going to do further studies and earn more money.

At that time, I came under a lot of pressure from family and friends. They said, "You are a doctor. You have a bright future before you." My father wanted me to specialize at the Cambridge University but I knew that the Lord had called me and I could not leave the ministry. My father-in-law even offered to help get me into a good department of the Teaching Hospital.

I always noticed the anxious and questioning look of my mother-in-law. My mother-in-law is very sweet and really cared about us. She was worried about both her daughter and me. I'm sure she thought I was destroying my life by refusing to pursue a lucrative and dignified medical career. One day the pressure was so much, I had to tell my dear concerned mother-in-law not to bring up the topic anymore.

At that time, our church was an unimpressive group of students and struggling Christians. A pastor's job has always been a controversial and disrespected profession. My father said to me, "What sort of job is this that pays by the collection of people's pennies? That is not an honourable way to live!"

I was under a lot of pressure. If I had yielded to the pressure of the people, perhaps all the souls who have been saved through this ministry would have perished. I am sure that there are people who are not in the ministry today because they listened to the voice of the people.

I have decided to ignore the voice of the people when I am sure that God wants me to do something. I may look controversial! I may displease people! But I am accountable to God for my calling. Woe is me if I preach not the Gospel!

People around say, "Do this" or "Do that"! They say to me, "You must have a hospital." Others tell me, "You must have a university!" Still others say, "You must travel more often to other churches." But what does God say?

Does God want me to use a million dollars to build a hospital or does He want me to use a million dollars to plant churches? I intend to do His will. You ensure that you do His will for your life and I'll make sure that I'm doing His will for mine! **The voice of the people is the voice that drowns the voice of the Holy Spirit.**

There are many ladies who yield to the voice of the people. "Why are you a virgin at this age? Enjoy yourself and have some fun!" They will put pressure on you to marry an unbeliever. "He's a good guy. If you marry him you will be happy." But the silent voice of the Word of God tells you not to be unequally yoked with unbelievers.

I know some associate pastors who are told by the congregation members, "You are a great pastor. I only enjoy coming to church when you are preaching." The voice of the people is telling them, "If you were your own boss and not an assistant, you would do very well in ministry." Perhaps they would do very well in ministry. Perhaps God is calling them to a great new work. **But make sure that it is the voice of the Holy Spirit that you follow and not the voice of the people.**

Some Jezebel-like wives tell their husbands, "You could have a nice car and a lot of money if you broke away from this tyrant of a General Overseer." "Come on," they say, "Do your own thing!" The voice of a wife is a very strong voice. It takes a very principled man to stay on course when his wife is prodding him to flow in another direction.

Never forget this! The voice of the people is the voice that drowns the voice of the Holy Spirit. It was not they who called you into the ministry! People cannot bless you! People cannot promote you! If you follow what people say, you will have to look to people for promotion. **But promotion does not come from people, it comes from the Lord.**

For promotion cometh neither from the east, nor from the west, nor from the south. But God is the judge: he putteth down one, and setteth up another.

Psalm 75:6,7

Not only are people powerless to help you, but they often turn against you after a while. Do you remember how people hailed Jesus as the Messiah on Palm Sunday? Just a few days later the same people screamed, "Crucify Him!" The people who hailed Him, did a one hundred and eighty degree turnaround and murdered Him.

Do not let the voice of friends or family come up higher than the voice of the Spirit of God.

Chapter 23

How Not to Be Led by Circumstances

...and the care of this world, and the deceitfulness of riches, choke the word, and he becometh unfruitful.

Matthew 13:22

The word circumstance is self-explanatory. "Circum" speaks of things around and "stances" speaks of things standing. **Therefore, "circumstances" simply mean "things standing around in your life".** These circumstances could be school, marriage, work or any situational factors.

Circumstances often dictate what Christians should do. **We are to be led by the Spirit of God and not by circumstances.** You cannot allow the circumstances in your life to prevent you from doing what you must do.

When I became a medical student, I had very little time to do the work of God. The circumstances were such that it was almost impossible for me to pray or read my Bible. But what was the silent voice of the Word of God telling me? The Word of God was telling me to be steadfast, unmovable and always abounding in the work of the Lord.

Therefore, my beloved brethren, BE YE STEDFAST, UNMOVEABLE, ALWAYS ABOUNDING in the work of the Lord, forasmuch as ye know that your labour is not in vain in the Lord.

1 Corinthians 15:58

And that is exactly what I did. The circumstances of a medical student were well known to other students. Because of this, medical students were not allowed to be leaders of the Christian fellowship. They knew that the circumstances of a medical student's life did not allow for much spiritual activity.

You see, we were picked up by a bus at 7:00 a.m. everyday and shuttled to the Teaching Hospital, about an hour's drive away. We stayed there all day until the evening. When we returned to the university campus at about 6:00 p.m., we were exhausted and had a lot of academic work to do.

How on earth could one be a useful Christian leader and at the same time pass the medical exams? But the good news is that I was able to do it by the grace of God. In my first year, I started a Christian ministry on the university campus. That ministry is still there today! During my fourth year, I established a church that has grown into a worldwide ministry.

There are many Christians who are led by circumstances. That is why they fall away from the Lord. The cares of this world (circumstances) quench the call!

...and the care of this world, and the deceitfulness of riches, choke the word, and he becometh unfruitful.

Matthew 13:22

God calls many people. However, the call of many is quenched by the circumstances of life. Many people are unfruitful today not because they are evil. **They are unfruitful because the voice of circumstances prevailed over the voice of the Spirit.**

When you have a baby, you are saddled with a real stressful schedule. It is up to you to rise above the circumstances and pray. Are you telling me that having a baby is a curse? Are you telling me that being married is a curse? If it is not a curse to you why do you allow these new circumstances to quench the zeal you once had? Rise up today in the name of Jesus. Rise above the voice of your circumstances.

God has called you to do great things in this life. **It is only great men who rise above the voice of circumstances.**

Chapter 24

How to Unmask the Devil

And the devil said unto him…

Luke 4:3

Our Lord Jesus was spoken to by the devil. Satan spoke to Him about three different topics. If you think that Satan will never speak to you, then you are joking. The devil tempts and tests everyone.

Jesus taught, "A servant is not above his master." If He was tempted, then we will also be tempted. It is easy to summarize the works of the devil into one word - *deception* The devil is a liar and a deceiver. Jesus called him the father of liars.

illusions, trickery

[handwritten note: I must always identify the area of my life in which I have become decieved.]

Ye are of your father the devil, and the lusts of your father ye will do. He was a murderer from the beginning, and abode not in the truth, because there is no truth in him. When he speaketh a lie, he speaketh of his own: FOR HE IS A LIAR, AND THE FATHER OF IT.

John 8:44

The Bible describes Satan as someone who deceives the whole world. Anyone who can deceive the entire world must be a very good liar and deceiver.

...that old serpent, called the Devil, and Satan, which deceiveth the whole world:...

Revelation 12:9

[handwritten note: Deception is the belief in a lie, or something that is never true.]

I know some politicians who have been able to deceive the masses. Some of them are able to deceive tribes and regions of a country. But to deceive the whole world is an awesome achievement. This means that all the intelligent and wise people have been taken in by the lie.

If you visit Europe today, you will see millions of people who believe that there is no God. They sincerely think that religion is not practical. They believe that life is all on this earth and that when you die you are dead like a dog. It is not a few people who hold this concept. These ideas are held by multitudes of intelligent but deceived Europeans.

Satan has managed to captivate the minds and hearts of this world with gold, silver and pleasure. Even when the realities of death and life dawn on people at funerals, the intellectuals of this world still refuse to acknowledge the existence of God.

Satan will produce a counterfeit to anything that God does in an attempt to deceive us. If the Holy Spirit gives dreams,

Satan will also come up with his own dreams. If God speaks in an audible voice, Satan will also give audible voices to confuse and deceive you. That is why the Bible says there are many voices in the world and none of them is without signification.

There are, it may be, so many kinds of voices in the world, and none of them is without signification.

1 Corinthians 14:10

The devil may open doors to deceive you. Satan also tries to close certain doors in your life. That is why Jesus is described as the one who can open the door that no one can ever close. That is what distinguishes the opening of a door by Jesus and the opening of a door by someone else.

...he that openeth, and no man shutteth; and shutteth, and no man openeth;

Revelation 3:7

If God has opened a door for you to marry Araba-Lucy, you will marry her. Nothing can stop it and nothing can change it! If God has determined that you should be a pastor over thousands of people, the wicked lies of your detractors cannot close that open door. If God has determined that you should be a millionaire in His kingdom, the economic circumstances around will not stop the blessings of God.

Our main job is to be able to decipher the deceptive traps and lies of the enemy. The Bible never teaches that we should beware of the power of the devil. Satan's strength is not in his power. In fact, he is powerless against you.

That is why God's instruction to us is to be careful of his tricks and lying traps.

Put on the whole armour of God, that ye may be able to stand against the <u>wiles</u> [deception, tricks, lies] of the devil.

<u>Note</u> it says wiles, not power or strength.   **Ephesians 6:11**

• Anything that makes you turn away from the word of God, even in the slightest is a deception!

• I must check <u>everything</u> with the word.

• There are no steps or warnings to deception, it just happens, that is why we must be filled with the word to identify our deception.

• self-righteousness is one of the greatest deceptions! Everybody else is rather more decieved than yourself! mercy!

Chapter 25

Three Checks to Avoiding Mistakes When Being Led by the Spirit

How do we fight against lying voices? There are three safety checks you must adhere to. This is to rule out the possibility of listening to the wrong voice.

Rule out the possibility of following the voice of your flesh by being honest with yourself. Admit to yourself when you realize that your flesh is influencing you. Remember that to be carnally minded is death.

Three Important Safety Checks

■ The safety of a multitude of counsellors

...in the multitude of counsellors there is safety.

Proverbs 11:14

There is nothing like the safety of counselling. If you have had a revelation from God, subject it to many counsellors (there is a difference between a counsellor and a friend). When you subject your revelations to a multitude of counsellors, you expose yourself to more information that helps you to take better decisions.

One aspiring pastor wanted to marry a young lady in the church. He prayed for several hours about whom he should marry. He finally came up with a decision and said that God had told him to marry a certain lady. Just before he proposed to the young lady, he decided to consult with an elder and with his pastor.

The elder said to him, "She's a nice girl. I see nothing wrong with your entering a relationship with this Christian lady."

Then, as a matter of formality, he decided to mention it to his pastor. When he did, the pastor said, "Oh, I see. She is a nice lady, however, I want you to be aware of one important thing."

He told the aspiring suitor, "This young lady has a severe mental disease. I prayed for her myself when she developed the condition."

The pastor went on, "As far as I know, she is still taking medication to control the effects of this condition."

He continued, "Of course, this does not bar you from marrying her. However, it is important for you to be aware of this reality before you take a decision."

The young man was taken aback, "Oh, I didn't know this!" he exclaimed.

He told the pastor, "Thank you very much. It will help me to take an informed decision."

This young man's safety depended on his consulting with more than one counsellor. The first counsellor (the elder) had nothing contrary to say. It was the second counsellor (the pastor) who had very important facts that the man needed to know.

You can see from this true-life story that the safety of this young man lay in the multitude of counsellors. There is no revelation, voice or instruction from God that cannot be subjected to a multitude of counsellors.

This is the reason why married couples must undergo extensive counselling. Many people who are getting married don't know the realities that are ahead of them. They have no idea about the journey that they are about to undertake. Their safety lies in the multitude of counsellors.

■ Prove all things

Prove all things; hold fast that which is good.

1 Thessalonians 5:21

Has a prophet spoken to you? Have you received a personal prophecy? Have you heard a voice from God? Please subject it to the test of the Word of God. Please prove *all* voices that you claim to have heard from God.

I sometimes operate in the prophetic gift. When I have a word of knowledge about someone, I often ask the individual concerned about the word I have received. I want to see if it is true and accurate because I know that I could be wrong. When a so-called prophet gives you a word of knowledge to leave your husband for another, please submit it to the Word of God.

Is it not the Word of God that tells us not to divorce? How could it be that a prophetic voice is speaking contrary to the Word of God?

Prophets Can Make Mistakes

A prophet prophesied to two of my leaders who were about to become pastors. He told them that within a year they would be living outside Ghana. He went on to tell them that they would be in the ministry but it would not be under the banner of Lighthouse Chapel International. These pastors were confused and wondered whether the Lord had spoken or not!

A year passed and these pastors were no nearer to going abroad than I was to the moon. After two years, it was quite clear that this prophecy had not materialized.

They have rather become pastors who are established in Lighthouse Chapel International in Ghana. The passage of time proved that this was either a mistaken prophet or a mistaken prophecy. Prophets are human, and they also make mistakes.

But the prophet, which shall presume to speak a word in my name, WHICH I HAVE NOT COMMANDED HIM TO SPEAK, or that shall speak in the name of other gods, even that prophet shall die. When a prophet speaketh in the name of the LORD, if the thing follow not, nor come to pass, that is the thing which the LORD hath not spoken, but THE PROPHET HATH SPOKEN IT PRESUMPTUOUSLY: thou shalt not be afraid of him.

Deuteronomy 18:20,22

All **prophets, prophecies, revelations and voices must be proved.** We must hold on to what is good. If you swallow every prophecy, revelation and dream, hook, line and sinker, you will soon find yourself gobbling down garbage.

When Paul received the call and revelation from God, he subjected it to a valid test. Paul had more revelations than any of the prophets we have around today, but notice how he practised this safety principle.

But when it pleased God, who separated me from my mother's womb, and called me by his grace, To reveal his Son in me, that I might preach him among the heathen; immediately I conferred not with flesh and blood: Neither went I up to Jerusalem to them which were apostles before me; but I went into Arabia, and returned again unto Damascus.

Galatians 1:15-17

Paul received a revelation from God. He did not confer with flesh and blood. The revelation was directly from the Lord. But after several years, look at how Paul subjected his revelation to the scrutiny of senior apostles. If you don't want

116

trouble, follow the principles that Paul practised and you will experience a sound and balanced ministry.

Then fourteen years after I went up again to Jerusalem with Barnabas, and took Titus with me also. And I went up by revelation, AND COMMUNICATED UNTO THEM THAT GOSPEL WHICH I PREACH AMONG THE GENTILES, BUT PRIVATELY TO THEM WHICH WERE OF REPUTATION, LEST BY ANY MEANS I SHOULD RUN, OR HAD RUN, IN VAIN.

Galatians 2:1,2

Paul received a revelation from God in Arabia. But he subjected his revelation to the scrutiny of Peter and other apostles who were of reputation. This is your key to safety in a minefield where there are many dangerous voices.

■ The confirmation of two witnesses

...In the mouth of two or three witnesses shall every word be established.

2 Corinthians 13:1

God has set a standard in His Word. It says that the mouth of two or more witnesses establishes a thing. **God's safety rule is simple: do not accept it unless a second witness confirms it.**

If a prophet gives a "word", you may ask, "Who is the second witness?" **The second witness can be you.** The prophecy can confirm something that God has already spoken to you about.

Even when it comes to dreams, a second dream helps to

confirm the message that came in the first dream. Notice how Joseph applied this principle when he was interpreting dreams for Pharaoh.

And for that the dream was doubled unto Pharaoh twice; it is because the thing is established by God, and God will shortly bring it to pass.

Genesis 41:32

The principle of confirmation by two witnesses is an important safety check for everyone who desires to safely experience the voice of God's direction for his life.

Chapter 26

Why You Must Listen to Your Conscience

God has given everybody a conscience. The conscience is that quiet inner voice that checks us when we go wrong. In charismatic circles, we hardly hear anything about the conscience. Your conscience is that quiet voice within that tells you when you are doing something wrong.

There are times when your heart (spirit) condemns you for doing something wrong.

For if OUR HEART CONDEMN US, God is greater than our heart, and knoweth all things. Beloved, if our heart condemn us not, then have we confidence toward God.

1 John 3:20,21

Your heart has the ability to condemn you for wrongdoing. It is only when your heart is not condemning you that you have confidence to approach God. The confidence comes because you know that you are doing the right thing. Pastors will do well to follow their consciences in the ministry. Christians will do well to follow the voice of their conscience. Apostle Paul said that he always tried to maintain a good conscience.

> **And herein do I exercise myself, to have always a CONSCIENCE VOID OF OFFENCE toward God, and toward men.**
>
> Acts 24:16

Any Christian who decides to follow his conscience will end up being a moral and upright person before the Lord. David prayed that God should keep him in the path of righteousness. **Your conscience is the instrument by which God will keep you in the path of righteousness**. Anyone who claims to be led by the Spirit or by prophets, but does not listen to the voice of his conscience is doomed to tragedy in life and ministry.

As you continue to ignore the voice of your conscience, it becomes deadened and hardened. This is what Paul described as having your conscience seared.

> **Speaking lies in hypocrisy; having their CONSCIENCE SEARED with a hot iron;**
>
> 1 Timothy 4:2

One minister was having an affair with one of his members. The lady asked him, "Pastor, how will you be able to preach tomorrow?" He laughed and said, "Oh, when I commit fornication I feel the anointing flowing even more."

This minister was used to committing immoral sins. It was now part and parcel of his life and ministry. *His conscience was no longer condemning him.* His conscience had become hardened. He now thought that sin was funny and made jokes about how the anointing was enhanced by fornication.

As soon as you make a mistake, respond to the voice of your heart condemning you. It will cause you to repent and get in line. After some years of neglecting your conscience, you will make shipwreck of your ministry. Shipwreck simply means disaster!

Holding faith, and a good conscience; which SOME HAVING PUT AWAY concerning faith have made SHIPWRECK:

1 Timothy 1:19

I have watched ministers who ignored their consciences. The end of such ministries is one and the same–shipwreck! This is why you must be careful about the thoughts you allow into your mind. If you permit certain thoughts, they will lead to other developments. **This is why you must be careful about telling lies, however small they are.**

Keep your conscience clear! Let your heart prick you whenever you are wrong! The voice of your conscience will lead you safely on the path of righteousness. I pray for you that you will live this life with the benefit of God's direction. I see you enjoying divine guidance as you apply the principles in this book to your everyday life!

May the Lord bless you as you follow the voice of God into success and victory! Follow His voice to the top because that is God's plan for you!

Other Best-Selling Books by Dag Heward-Mills

*Loyalty and Disloyalty

Leaders and Loyalty

Ministering with Signs and Wonders

Transform Your Pastoral Ministry

The Art of Leadership

Model Marriage

Church Planting

*The Megachurch

*Lay People and the Ministry

*These titles are also available in Spanish and French. Information about other foreign translations of some of the titles above may be obtained by writing to our address.

For additional information on Dag Heward-Mills' books, tapes and ideos write to these addresses:

Dag Heward-Mills
P. O. Box KB114
Korle-Bu, Accra
Ghana, West-Africa

Website:

www.daghewardmills.org

Email:

bishop@daghewardmills.org

evangelist@daghewardmills.org

About the Author

One night, whilst still a medical student, the Lord anointed Dag Heward-Mills as he waited on Him in a remote town of Ghana. He was supernaturally anointed and heard the words "from now on you can teach..." This supernatural call is what has ushered him into a worldwide ministry.

Today, his Healing Jesus Crusades are conducted throughout the world with thousands in attendance and many accompanying miracles. These phenomenal miracles, attested to by medical doctors, have included the opening of the eyes of the blind, the restoring of hearing to the deaf, the emptying of wheel chairs and even the raising of the dead.

Dag Heward-Mills, an author of several best selling books, also founded the Lighthouse Chapel International which has become a worldwide denomination. His radio, TV and internet programs reach millions around the world. Other outreaches include pastors and ministers conferences and the renowned Anagkazo Bible Ministry & Training Centre.